Phips' Amphibious Assault on Canada – 1690

Origins, Logistics, and Organization

The Attack and Aftermath

&

'Where Sovereignty Lay'

Robert W. Passfield

For

Susan James

In appreciation of her understanding
and support as my retirement years
continue to be devoted to a demanding
muse – Clio – in the writing of history.

© 2011. Robert W. Passfield. All rights reserved.

No part of this book may be reproduced, stored in a retrieval system, or transmitted by any means without the written permission of the author.

ISBN - 10: 1463790007

ISBN - 13: 9781463790004

LCCN - 2011909696

Summary: This book comprises a narrative history of the origins, conduct, and aftermath of the Phips' Canada Expedition of 1690, as well as a political treatise on 'where sovereignty lay' within the context of the historical evolution of the constitutional struggle over sovereignty in the Massachusetts Bay Colony. It treats the history of the Canada Expedition within the context of the worldview and religious frame of mind of the Massachusetts Puritans, and their particular hopes and fears, at a time when New England was suffering from devastating attacks by the French and their Indian allies and undergoing a political upheaval with the Crown and the Colony at odds over 'where sovereignty lay'.

- Phips' Canada Expedition
- amphibious assault
- Puritan mind
- sovereignty
- Sir William Phips

Cover Design: Craig Passfield

Contents

Preface ... vii

Acknowledgements ... xiii

Chapter One: Origins, Logistics, and Organization ... 1

Chapter Two: The Attack and Aftermath ... 33

Chapter Three: 'Where Sovereignty Lay' ... 75

Bibliography ... 145

Index ... 151

A Note about the Author ... 159

Maps

New York, New England, Acadia, and Canada, ca. 1690. (Ken Watson, 2011) 2

Quebec under siege by New Englanders, October 1690. (Harvard Map Collection, 1855) 34

Tracing of "Plan de Québec et de ses environs, en la Nouvelle France, assiégé par les Anglais, octobre 1690 ...", Sr. de Villeneuve, ingénieur du Roy, [ca. 1692].

Mainland English Colonies of North America, ca. 1690. (Ken Watson, 2011) 76

Preface

This publication is based on research conducted some time ago by the author in providing historical research support to a Parks Canada archaeological excavation of a 17th century shipwreck; a shipwreck that turned out to be a lost ship of the Sir William Phips' fleet that sailed from Boston in August 1690 to attack Quebec.

In support of the archaeology project the author prepared two manuscripts: a historical narrative on the origins, logistics, and conduct of the Phips' Canada Expedition of 1690; and a treatise on "Where Sovereignty Lay' to determine whether or not the Crown of England held sovereign power over the existing charter government of the Massachusetts Bay Colony at the time of the Phips' Canada Expedition.

Subsequently the historical manuscript was divided into two article-length works, and all three pieces have been revised, expanded, and re-cast to form the chapters of this book.

Background

In December 1994, a submerged shipwreck was discovered in shallow water on the north shore of the St. Lawrence River at Baie Trinité, just downstream from the City of Baie Comeau, Quebec; and three years later, in 1996-1997, the site was excavated, recorded, and documented by the Underwater Archaeology Service, Ontario Region, Parks Canada Agency. An analysis of the wrecked vessel and recovered artefacts revealed that the ship was from the squadron of Sir William Phips that had sailed from Boston in August 1690 to attack New France (Canada).

From the historical record it was known that four vessels were lost by Sir William Phips on his return voyage, following an unsuccessful assault on Quebec, but the name of the wrecked vessel in the St. Lawrence River was initially a mystery. Thereafter initials found on several of the conserved artefacts, in conjunction with research in archival records pertaining to the personnel of the several missing militia companies of the expedition, established that the wrecked ship was transporting the Dorchester Company of Dorchester, Massachusetts.[1]

Further research in primary documents from the Massachusetts Archives and contemporary historical accounts, enabled the wrecked ship to be identified as a lost victualler of the Phips' fleet – the *Elizabeth and Mary*, a 45-ton bark commanded by Captain Caleb Lamb.[2] During that research effort the author was assigned to prepare a study of the Phips' Canada Expedition to provide a historical context for interpretation purposes, where the shipwreck and the recovered artefacts were concerned.

In pursuing research in primary sources a strict attention was paid to meeting particular programme needs through: identifying the known participants, and the names and types of ships in the expedition; in tracing the origins of the expedition, its organization, logistics, and conduct; and in ascertaining the challenges of the ocean voyage, and the military tactics adopted in the attack on Quebec and its failure. In addition, a particular attention was paid to the return voyage and the losses suffered including the names of the lost ships and their respective fates in so far as that could be determined from the historical record.

Information was also sought on how the soldiers and sailors were recruited, the terms of their service, and the terms under which the ships were engaged, and in whose service. Attention was paid as well to ascertaining what provisions were made to cover the loss of a ship and its contents while engaged in the Canada Expedition, and what payment of compensation, if any, was made for the loss of a ship and its contents, and what that entailed.

Historical Approach

At this point a comment is requisite on the nature of this publication, which differs from a conventional academic history monograph. The book comprises three distinct, but related pieces, the first two of which comprise simply an historical narrative of the origins, logistics, and conduct of the Phips' Canada Expedition from its inception to its wind up. They describe and relate, in a chronological order, the story of what transpired as recorded by the New England participants who left a record of their particular views and involvement in the event.

In sum, no particular argument is being presented within an historiographical context, and no claim is being made to advancing any new interpretation. There is little analysis or weighing of the New Englanders' motives for attacking New France, nor any elaboration of the meaning and significance of the event itself within the history of the imperial conflict between England and France in North America during King William's War (1689-1697), or more broadly within the historical context of the wars of survival endured by international Protestantism in a late 17th Century context. And more particularly, there is no analysis of what the failed expedition ultimately accomplished, or contributed, to the English cause in the war with France and her Indian allies.

Although an historian by profession, the author has declined to play the role of the 'objective' historian bent on interpreting the broader meaning of the event and informing the reader of what conclusions to draw. Readers are left to sort out their own thoughts, judgements, and dare we say feelings, about the Canada Expedition in all its various aspects, and to form their own interpretations as to what ultimately motivated the Phips' expedition amongst a mix of possible motives.

Was the Canada Expedition purely the product of a military strategy to put an end to the devastating French and Indian raids on the New England frontier that were causing an increasingly heavy loss of life and suffering, or were there more diverse and deeper motives? Was the expedition motivated by a desire for plunder; a religious zeal to defend Protestantism or simply to smote the Catholics; or a patriotic drive to strike a blow against a traditional enemy, France, with whom the mother country was engaged in a struggle for the survival of Protestantism? On the other hand, was the expedition motivated simply by a hope for economic gain in seeking to expand fishing areas and trade at the expense of the French? Or did the New England Puritans act from a mix of these various motives?

For the founders of the Massachusetts Bay Colony any attempt to analyze and weigh the various possible motives behind their actions, would be pointless. The founders possessed a coherent worldview shaped by their theology; and their actions were motivated by, and guided by, a religious frame of mind: their faith, their religious beliefs, and their intellectual and emotional involvement in the struggles of international Calvinism and Protestantism in England and Europe, both theological and military.

For the founders, imperial, economic, and religious matters were 'all of a piece' pursued within the context of a sense of participating in a Holy War in defence of international Calvinism and Protestantism against the Catholic powers.[3] However, the extent to which the leaders of the Massachusetts Bay Colony had become 'Americanized' by the close of the 17th Century, and more concerned and motivated by domestic issues, remains a moot point.

Ironically, the only decided interpretation being proffered by the author in this historical narrative is the general statement, unsupported by any comparative analysis, that the seaborne assault on Canada was an unprecedentedly stupendous undertaking for any colony at the end of the 17th Century. That broad statement of interpretation is based simply on the author's general knowledge of colonial history.

The chapters were written from the viewpoint of the leading political, military, and religious leaders of the Massachusetts Bay Colony who left a record of how they, themselves, conceptualized, and sought to explain, understand, and justify the Phips' amphibious assault on Canada and its devastating outcome, within the framework of the theology and world view of the Massachusetts Puritans, and their belief in Providence.

As such it is not a social history of the Phips' Expedition written from the viewpoint of the common man, rather it conveys the views of the elite of the colony. It is also a story of the organizational and logistical difficulties, and the challenges faced, in carrying out an amphibious operation over hundreds of miles of open sea and unchartered river waters in the age of sail, combined with a tale of the resultant cost in human lives and suffering, and the impact of disease.

In sum, no claim is being made to having produced a balanced historical account that illuminates and seeks to understand and explain the views, actions, and outlook of both sides in the conflict, including those of the aboriginal participants. To the contrary, the story is related solely from one point of view: that of the leadership of the Massachusetts Bay Colony.

The third chapter, 'Where Sovereignty Lay', traces the long constitutional struggle of the 17th Century between the Crown and the Massachusetts Bay Colony, and in particular the evolution of the Puritan interpretation of the Charter of 1629 as embodying a bestowal of sovereignty by the Crown on the Massachusetts Bay Company.

This particular study was undertaken to examine, within an historical context, the question of where sovereignty resided at the time of the Phips' Canada Expedition following the 'Glorious Revolution of 1688' in England and the overthrow by the colonists of the royal government of Sir Edmund Andros at Boston, in April 1689. More specifically, it sought, and seeks, to determine whether the Crown of England had any responsibility for the Phips' Expedition under the re-established charter form of colonial government as it existed in the Massachusetts Bay Colony following the re-forming of a political relationship with the dominion sovereign, the Crown, just nine months prior to the undertaking of the Phips' Canada Expedition.

In its entirety, this book is intended to appeal to the general reader with an interest in history, who enjoys reading narrative histories and/or pondering intellectual concepts. Hopefully, it will prove interesting and thought provoking.

---

1. R. James Ringer, "Phips' Fleet, missing for 304 Years", *National Geographic*, vol. 198, no. 2, August 2000, pp. 72-81; and *1690 The Siege of Québec, The Story of a Sunken Ship* (Montréal: Montréal Museum of History and Archaeology, 2000), which catalogues an exhibit of the recovered artifacts conserved by the Centre de conservation du Québec. Online report: *L'épave du Elizabeth and Mary (1690): Rapport d'activités 1997, Sous la direction de Marc-André Bernier* (Service d'archéologie subaquatique, Centre de Service de l'Ontario, Parcs Canada, Février 2008). The Centre de conservation du Québec was a co-sponsor, with the Parks Canada Agency, of the shipwreck excavation and was responsible for conserving many of the recovered artifacts.

2. When the physical evidence from the shipwreck failed to conclusively identify the name of the wrecked ship, historical documents from the Massachusetts Archives and contemporary 17th Century published works were consulted and analyzed to identify the vessel. That analysis was carried out by: Professor Emerson W. Baker, Salem State College, the co-author (with John G. Read) of *The New England Knight, Sir William Phips, 1651-1695* (Toronto: University of Toronto Press, 1998); Marc-André Bernier, Underwater Archaeology Service, Parks Canada; and Robert W. Passfield, Historical Services Branch, Parks Canada.

3. Perry Miller, *The New England Mind: From Colony to Province*, vol. 2 (Cambridge, Mass.: Harvard University Press, 1953), Prologue, p. 6.

Acknowledgements

As a graduate student in history, I was always fascinated with the concept that 'ideas influence actions'; and that history is much more than just a record of 'what happened' in a physical sense. What men actually did might well be the result of accident, of compromises forced on them by events beyond their control, or the opposite of what they intended through their actions having unforeseen consequences.

To truly understand and relate what the leaders of a community were seeking to accomplish, the historian must penetrate into the mind of the historical actors to comprehend their particular world view, and the matrix of political, cultural and moral values, as well as the theology, that underlay their thought processes. In effect, the historian must understand their particular beliefs and values, hopes and fears, and must know their particular circumstances as seen through their own eyes. What the leading actors in any historical action sought to achieve, and their approach to doing so, was ultimately guided and governed by how their peculiar situation was perceived and conceptualized within their own particular mental framework.

As a historian I have continued to be intrigued by the work of the American intellectual historian, and Professor of American Literature, Perry Miller (1905-1963), in his studies of the American historical experience from the beginning of settlement in New England. In particular what attracted me to Miller's work was his assertion that the Puritans had a coherent worldview, which was based on their theology and guided and governed their actions; and that the history of the establishment and development of the Massachusetts Bay Colony was an effort to work out their religious ideals in action.

For example, in *The New England Mind: From Colony to Province* (1953) Miller treats, in an historical narrative, the interaction of the religious ideals of the Puritans with the realities of the North

American environment. He relates the history of a struggle which ultimately resulted in the "City upon a Hill" that the Puritan founders were striving to establish, evolving into a materialistic society contrary to their best intentions and efforts. More generally, I concur with Perry Miller's exclamation concerning his view of history:

> "I have difficulty imagining that anyone can be a historian without realizing that history itself is part of the life of the mind; hence I have been compelled to insist that the mind of man is the basic factor in human history."[1]

Where the actual practice of writing history is concerned, I have found much of value in the precepts of Barbara Tuchman (1912-1989). In graduate school, I read Tuchman's book *The Guns of August* (1962), and immediately sought out and consulted her views on the craft of writing history as presented in a volume of published pieces: *Practicing History, Selected Essays*. The general precepts that guided Tuchman's particular approach to the writing of history may be categorized as follows:

Research: Consult secondary sources on your subject for a general overview, but base your research and writing on primary sources which are much more immediate and revealing of character and circumstance than material that has been preselected by someone else for a particular purpose; and make yourself acquainted with the geography and topography of the area where the event took place to understand the distances and the nature and features of the terrain, which, when conveyed to a reader, makes the history more graphic, intelligible, and real;

Writing: Select the essential and relevant material from primary sources, distill and make sense of it, and assemble the material in the form of "a developing dramatic narrative"; enhance readability by paying attention to the sound of words and the interaction of sound and sense, and by avoiding convoluted sentences and long multi-syllabic words; let the structure evolve naturally as the writing proceeds; and write "as of the time" in terms of what the actors knew and understood themselves, and avoid the insertion of comments based on knowledge gained in hindsight that would not have been known at the time;

Interpretation: Focus on the history of the particular event under study, rather than on an explanation of the meaning of the event; let the presentation of the material in the historical narrative tell the story, and do not impose an interpretation on the material; the interpretation of the event is a collaboration between the author and the reader with the author presenting what happened and the reader drawing conclusions as to 'why' it happened as it did, in an interactive exercise.

The ultimate goal for Tuchman was to write a clear, interesting, and highly readable narrative history for the general reader, and to enthrall the reader by producing a dramatic story that would appeal to the emotions as well as the intellect. In sum, Tuchman thought of herself "as a storyteller, a narrator, who deals in true stories, not fiction"; and one can readily understand what attracted her to the particularly dramatic historical events and historical periods that she treated in her major books.[2]

As an historian by training and profession, the author has an appreciation and understanding of the role of the historian in the writing of history beyond that of an accomplished storyteller. Yet, that being said, there is much of value for the historian in Barbara Tuchman's precepts for the writing of history, and there are past events that do lend themselves to a narrative history treatment. Such a past event is, in the judgement of the author, the Phips' Canada Expedition of 1690.

Within the chapters of this book, two distinct approaches are in evidence with respect to the research and writing of history. In the first two chapters, "Origins, Logistics, and Organization" and "The Attack and Aftermath", Barbara Tuchman's general precepts concerning the writing of history were followed. The story of the Phips' Canada Expedition is based on primary research, and records the outlook, and the immediate fears and concerns, of the New England Puritan leadership at the time of the undertaking. It expounds as well on the organization and conduct of the expedition as seen through the eyes of the Puritans, and their explanation for its failure.

In undertaking the research and writing of the third chapter, "Where Sovereignty Lay", the author was guided by Perry Miller's assertion that "history itself is the life of the mind". A deliberate effort was made to convey the evolution of the sovereignty issue in 17th Century New England in terms of: how it was conceived and understood within the broad context of the theology and world view of the New England Puritans; and how their religious doctrines and beliefs underlay their constitutional arguments and political actions, as well as their perception and understanding of their situation.

Although both Miller and Tuchman had an influence on the research and writing of the chapters in this particular book, any deficiencies in the conceptualization and treatment of the subject and/or the writing of the historical narrative and treatise, are solely the responsibility of the author.

Within the historical narrative there are instances of a blending of voice, or persona, with the author and the Puritans appearing to speak as one, in the same voice. This is a product of the author's effort to enter into the Puritan mind to understand and convey, as immediately as possible, the views, feelings and apprehensions of the Puritans regarding their situation, for which no apology is offered.

Perry Miller has noted the challenge that the historian faces in seeking to present the beliefs and doctrines of the Puritans in their own terms, and to make them comprehensible regardless of whether they are palatable to our contemporaries. "Respect for them is not the same thing as believing in them".[3] To which one might add, likewise, that when an historian expounds on a particular view of events as seen through the eyes of his historical

Acknowledgements

subjects – in this case, Puritan eyes – it does not mean that the historian necessarily shares their views or their prejudices.

On a personal level, I am greatly indebted to a good friend, Ken Watson, who prepared the maps for this publication, and to my nephew, Craig Passfield, who designed the book covers. Their respective contributions are much appreciated. An especial thanks is owed as well to my brother, John Passfield, for perusing and commenting in detail on the manuscript. His comments have resulted in an improved clarity.

Although the chapters of this book, *Phips' Amphibious Assault on Canada – 1690,* are based on manuscripts prepared initially by the author while employed as a public historian by the Parks Canada Agency of the Canadian Government, the author is solely responsible for the present content and presentation. It is offered to the public in the belief that a narrative history of the Phips' Canada Expedition written from the viewpoint of the leading New England participants, together with a political thought treatise on the polity of the Massachusetts Bay Colony, will find a ready audience beyond the realm of readers of academic histories.

The three chapters assembled in this book are examples of the 'applied history' approach utilized by Parks Canada in employing historical research, and historical research methodologies and analysis to investigate, and resolve, particular questions raised during the carrying out of a heritage conservation and interpretation project. The historical treatment in evidence in the present work is also illustrative of the author's belief that 'ideas influence actions'.

Hopefully, the insights provided into the theological frame of mind and worldview of the Puritans of the Massachusetts Bay Colony, and the circumstances in which they found themselves at the time of the undertaking of the Phips' Canada Expedition, will prove of more than a passing interest in revealing "the thought behind their acts".[4]

Lastly, I am indebted to the history graduate school at McMaster University which, long ago, imbued me with a lasting interest in intellectual history, political philosophy, and historiography.

Robert W. Passfield
Ottawa, Ontario, Canada
March 2011

---

1. Perry Miller, *Errand into the Wilderness* (New York: Harper Torchbooks, 1964), Preface, p. ix.

2. Barbara Tuchman, *Practicing History, Selected Essays* (New York: Alfred A. Knopf, 1981 edition). This summary of Tuchman's precepts for the writing of history was prepared from the following pieces: pp. 13-24, "In Search of History" (May 1963); pp. 25-32, "When Does History Happen?" (March 1964); pp. 33-44, "History by the Ounce" (July 1965); and pp. 45-50, "The Historian as Artist" (March 1966). The storyteller quote is from p. 18.

3. Miller, *Errand into the Wilderness*, Preface, p. ix.

4. This is a phrase borrowed from E.H. Carr, *What is History?*, ed. R.W. Davies (New York: Penguin Books, 1990 reprint), p. 24, wherein Carr comments on "the historian's need of imaginative understanding for the minds of the people with whom he is dealing, for the thought behind their acts".

Phips' Amphibious Assault on Canada – 1690

CHAPTER ONE

Origins, Logistics, and Organization

In 1690 the Massachusetts Bay Colony mounted two major amphibious assaults, under the command of Sir William Phips, against the French territories in North America. Undertaken to conquer Acadia and Canada, the expeditions were successive phases in a concerted plan to put an end to a series of devastating attacks which were launched against New England by the French of Canada and their Indian allies.

Born of desperation and a fear for the very survival of the Massachusetts Bay Colony, the two military expeditions constituted an amazing achievement for a colonial government in the magnitude of the enterprise, and distances covered, as well as in the organizational and logistical challenges overcome; yet ultimately the effort to conquer Canada ended in an unmitigated disaster.

Chapter One sets forth the origins, logistics, and organization of the Phips' Canada Expedition, and includes an historical overview of the Acadia Expedition (April-May 1690) which constituted the first stage in the projected conquest of Canada.

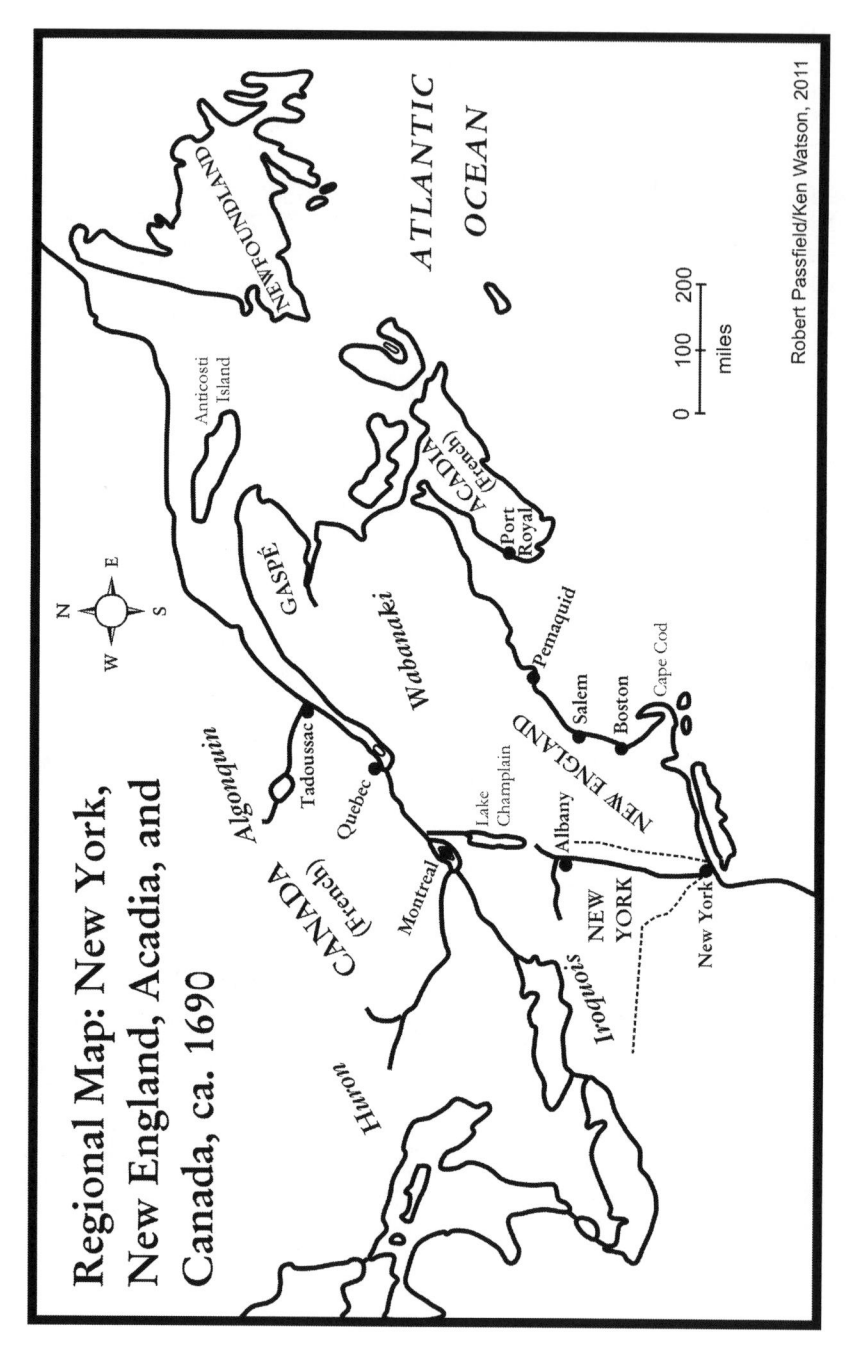

Map One

New York, New England, Acadia, and Canada, ca. 1690.
(Ken Watson, 2011)

Chapter One

Origins, Logistics, and Organization

From the founding of the Massachusetts Bay plantation by a royal charter in 1629, the colonial government had acted as a *de facto* sovereign power in governing the colony and defending its frontiers, virtually independent of the Crown. When at war with the Indians, it was the colonial charter government, the General Court, which planned campaigns, appointed officers, raised troops, and supplied them in the field.

The involvement of the English Crown was limited to supplying the colony with ordnance, gunpowder, and munitions for its general defence. This relationship had changed for only a brief period under the royal government of the Dominion of New England (1686-1689) which firmly established the sovereignty of the Crown over the colony and vested responsibility for defending the colony in a Commander-in-Chief appointed by the Crown, Sir Edmund Andros, the Royal Governor.

As Commander-in-Chief, Andros commanded military operations, appointed militia officers, raised militia units, and levied taxes on the colony in order to prosecute a costly and indecisive war with the Wabanaki Indians in Maine. However, following the overthrow of the Andros government by citizens of Boston in April 1689, the Massachusetts Bay Colony was once again solely responsible for its own defence. The former General Court government was no sooner re-established, and recognized as a provisional government by the Crown, than the colony came under attack by the French and their Indian allies.

The Acadia Expedition, April-May 1690

Where military matters were concerned, the re-established General Court had initially confined its activities to defending the colony's eastern frontiers against attack by the Wabanaki Indians, but this changed as of December 1689 with the receipt of news of the outbreak of war between England and France.

The French and their Indian allies from Canada launched devastating attacks against the northern New England frontier settlements, and French frigates from Port Royal cruised along the seacoast wreaking havoc among the colonies' fishing fleets and commercial shipping. Faced with a war on all fronts, the General Court of the Massachusetts Colony became convinced that the only effective way of defending the colony against the French and their Indian allies was to take the offensive against French bases in Acadia and, if successful, to ultimately attack and conquer Canada.

Initially, the General Court decided to attack Port Royal, and the other French outposts in Acadia, in an effort to protect the Atlantic fishery and commercial coastal shipping.[1] Unable to finance a naval expedition owing to the heavy costs of the war against the Indians on the frontier, the General Court called for volunteers among the wealthy citizens and merchants of Boston to undertake the expedition as a private enterprise, and appointed a committee of merchants to advize on how the expedition might be organized and financed.[2]

Subsequently, the recommendations contained in the report of the committee were incorporated into a decree of the General Court that offered any entrepreneurs willing to undertake to finance and carry out an expedition against Acadia a grant of a series of rights and authorities to support and compensate them: permission to raise volunteers in the colony; commissions from the General Court for all officers needed for the expedition; the loan of two warships from the colony's coastal patrol; the sole control and profit of the trade of Acadia, until the Crown should decide on its future disposal; and all captured plunder, with the exception of large artillery which was to be offered to the government of Massachusetts.

What the decree failed to offer was a financial guarantee to the promoters of the expedition. The report of the committee of merchants had recommended that the General Court agree to reimburse the private interests for any shortfall between the cost of the expedition and the monies retrieved through plunder and control of the Acadian trade should the territory be recaptured or their rights taken from them by the Crown before the captured trade yielded substantial returns.[3]

Without such a guarantee private interests were unwilling to hazard the financing of the Acadia expedition. The project languished until news arrived in late February that a war party of French and Indians had attacked and destroyed Schenectady, New York. Over 60 men, women, and children, were massacred, the settlement burned, and some twenty prisoners carried off to Quebec. This outrage roused the government to action in strengthening the frontier defences and convinced the General Court, despite the depleted state of its finances, to undertake offensive operations against the French wherever possible.[4]

On March 14, 1690, the General Court ordered that an expedition be undertaken against Acadia "at the publick Charge with all speed"; appointed a committee of magistrates to advise the General Court on the shipping, provisions, ammunitions, and stores, required for the expedition; and levied a tax to raise monies for immediate expenditures.[5] In addition, a committee of military officers was established and empowered to issue orders and impress vessels, sailors, and soldiers, should they fail to volunteer.

One of the members of the military committee, Sir William Phips, was designated by the General Court "to take Chief Command of all the Forces that shall be raised for that Expedition, Shipping, and Seamen employed therein", and the Court ordered that commissions be prepared for Sir William Phips, the Captains, and Commissioned Officers for both the land and sea forces. The Instructions for the expedition, and Articles of War, were also ordered be drawn up.[6]

To encourage soldiers to volunteer for service in the Acadia expedition, the General Court decreed that all volunteers would receive the regular militia pay; that the soldiers and their officers would share half of any plunder taken from the French; and that the wives and children of any volunteers lost in action would receive their pay and share of the plunder.[7]

The man appointed by the General Court to command the Acadia expedition, was well known to Bostonians. A resident of Boston, Phips was born February 2, 1651, on the eastern frontier of New England, in Maine, where his father, James Phips, a gunsmith and recent immigrant from Bristol, England, had cleared a farmstead in the forest along the Sheepscot River and engaged in trade with the Wabanaki Indians.

Following the death of his father, young Phips was apprenticed as a shipwright and subsequently practiced his trade in Boston. He married the widow of a Boston merchant, and while still a young man, he had contracted to construct a large ship of 117 tons at the family plantation on the Sheepscot River. However, his stay on the family farmstead was short lived.

In August 1676, the Wabanaki had launched a surprise attack on the Sheepscot and nearby Kennebec river settlements, and the occupants of the Phips' plantation had narrowly escaped death through sailing the newly-launched merchant ship to Boston. Having lost his family plantation, Phips sought subsequently to re-establish himself through searching for Spanish treasure ships that had been wrecked in the Caribbean, and achieved some success in recovering small amounts of Spanish silver.[8]

In 1683 Phips sailed for England where, through important family connections, he succeeded in gaining powerful sponsors at the Admiralty and Court to back a major treasure-seeking expedition. He was equipped with two ships, and granted a royal commission to search for and salvage wrecked Spanish galleons in the waters off Hispaniola, the Bahamas, and in the Gulf of Florida. Phips made two voyages to the Caribbean, and in January 1686/87 had discovered, in the shoals off the island of Hispaniola, the sunken wreck a Spanish galleon, the *Nuestra Señora de la Concepción*. Lost for some 45 years, it reputedly had one of the richest cargoes of any of the Spanish treasure ships lost in the West Indies. Over a period of four months, Phips' divers were able to recover some 30 tons of silver from the *Concepción* with a value of over £205,000.

On returning to England in June 1687, Phips had received £11,000 as his share of the undertaking, and a knighthood from King James II who retained a 10% royalty, over £20,000, as the Crown's share of the treasure. Phips had also received a Crown patronage appointment as Provost Marshall General in the newly-established royal government of the Dominion of New England, headed by Sir Edmund Andros.

As Provost Marshal General, Phips would be responsible for the appointment and supervision of sheriffs throughout the Dominion. However, when Phips arrived in Boston on June 1, 1688, he found that the sheriffs had already been appointed, and Governor Andros refused to dismiss them. Angry at being deprived of the patronage of his new office, Phips determined to seek redress in London.

On July 7, 1688, the day after being sworn in as Provost Marshall General, Phips sailed from Boston to London. Subsequently, he failed to gain an audience with the King, but became closely associated with the reverend Increase Mather of the Massachusetts Bay Colony. Mather had been sent to London to petition King James for the recall of Sir Edmund Andros and the restoration of the Massachusetts Bay Company Charter of 1629.

While Phips was in England, Prince William of Orange of the Dutch Republic (Republic of the United Netherlands) landed a Protestant army of 15,000 men in November 1688, and the Catholic King, James II, fled the country. And in January 1689, a "Convention Parliament" bestowed the English throne on Prince William and his wife Princess Mary, as joint sovereigns: King William III and Queen Mary.

Almost immediately Phips and Mather had begun to lobby the new Court and Parliament for a restoration of the Charter of the Massachusetts Bay Colony on which the colony's former government was based. The following month, Phips and Mather submitted a joint petition to the Lords of Trade charging that the Charter had been "taken away by illegal and arbitrary proceedings", and appeared together before the Lords of Trade to support their joint petition. However, that petition came to naught.

Phips returned to Boston on May 29, 1689, some six weeks after the April 1689 insurrection that had overthrown Sir Edmund Andros and the royal government of Dominion of New England. With the royal government being defunct, and his appointment as Provost Marshal General rendered meaningless, Phips did not participate actively in the political process that led to the establishment of a revolutionary popular government in the Massachusetts Bay Colony.

Phips was neither a member of the Puritan congregation, nor a freeman of the Colony of Massachusetts Bay, and hence, under the re-established charter government, he had no right to vote or stand for election to the General Court. However, his close association in London with the Puritan minister, Increase Mather, had stood him in good stead with the revolutionary government in Boston. Phips soon developed a close friendship with another leading Puritan divine, Cotton Mather, the minister of the North Church in Boston, and son of the Reverend Increase Mather.[9]

When differing views emerged in the re-established General Court over whom to appoint to command the expedition against Acadia, Sir William Phips offered his services.[10] In response, on March 22, 1690, the Governor and Council admitted Phips as a Freeman of the Colony, with all the rights and privileges pertaining thereto; empowered a committee to impress men for the Acadia expedition, "not exceeding Five Hundred in the whole"; and declared that:

"... the Honourable Sr. William Phipps Knt. having Voluntarily Offered Himself to that Service, is desired to take the Chief Command of all the Forces that shall be raised for that Expedition, Shipping, and Seamen employed therein."[11]

The very next day, March 23rd, 1690, he made a confession of faith, was baptized by Cotton Mather at the North Church in Boston, and admitted into the Puritan congregation.[12] Subsequently Phips was elected a magistrate, thereby joining the governing Council of the General Court provisional government of the Colony of Massachusetts Bay.[13]

While preparations were underway for the launching the Acadia expedition, and the entry of its commander into the governing Council of the General Court, word was received on March 19th of the destruction of Salmon Falls, New Hampshire. Thirty-four settlers had been killed by a war party of French and Indian marauders who had torched the settlement, slaughtered the cattle, and carried off some 50 women and children as prisoners to Quebec.

Thoroughly outraged, the Governor and Council immediately ordered that letters be sent to the governors of neighbouring colonies suggesting that they appoint commissioners to meet in New York to coordinate colonial defences, and devise ways to provide mutual assistance in resisting the attacks of the French and their Indian allies.[14]

On March 29th Governor Bradstreet sent a dispatch to the Secretary of State, the Earl of Shrewsbury, in London, England, on a fast-sailing vessel, the Sloop *Resolution*. The dispatch informed their Majesties, King William and Queen Mary, that despite the utmost efforts to defend their Majesties' colonies and plantations, they continued to be harassed and were under constant threat of attack by a force of five or six hundred French from Canada who had joined with the Indians in launching attacks against the frontier settlements of New England.

Efforts were underway to strengthen the frontier defences, but after due deliberation it was concluded that the most effective means of preventing further attack, and restoring a lasting peace, was to conquer and remove the French. Thus the Colony had resolved to mount an attack on Port Royal by sea, and if successful, God willing, had in contemplation an attack on Canada.

What was lacking was sufficient arms and ammunition to mount a major expedition against Canada, as at present there was barely sufficient ammunition to equip the Port Royal expedition. Hence, the General Court requested, as humble supplicants, that the Crown "countenance" the expeditions against Acadia and Canada, and afford them assistance with shipping, and through the speedy sending of arms and ammunition sufficient to defend themselves and resist the attacks of the enemy.[15]

While contemplating an assault against Canada, preparations continued for the expedition against Acadia. The Governor and Council appointed, and empowered, a committee to impress men for service should there not be enough volunteers; captains were commissioned to command the ships; and orders were given for the impressment of seamen. Instructions were also issued to Sir William Phips, the newly-appointed "Commander in Chiefe of all Sea, and Land Forces for the Eastern Expedition to Nova Scotia", to attack and capture Port Royal and other French outposts in Acadia.[16]

As of the spring of 1690 any attack against Canada was purely speculative pending the outcome of the Acadia expedition. However the meeting of the colonial commissioners, which was held in New York on May 1st to discuss common defence measures, brought a further development. The commissioners of Connecticut, Plymouth, Massachusetts and New York agreed that each colony would contribute to an 850-man force to defend Albany, which was believed to be under an immediate threat of attack, and they developed a strategic plan for a two-pronged attack against French settlements on the St. Lawrence River. Montreal would be attacked by a land force proceeding northwards from Albany; and, at the same time, Quebec would be assaulted by a seaborne force sailing northwards from Boston.[17]

The General Court acted immediately. An order was issued for 160 soldiers to be despatched to Albany to strengthen its defences and to participate in the projected attack on Montreal. Sixty men were also sent to Albany from the Plymouth Colony by Order of the General Court.[18] Further action would depend on news of the fate of the Acadia expedition.

Two weeks earlier, on April 28th, Sir William Phips had sailed from Boston for Acadia with a fleet of seven ships and 736 soldiers. He arrived opposite Port Royal on May 9th, and the next day issued an ultimatum demanding the surrender of the fort and garrison. Badly outnumbered and lacking mounted cannon to defend the fort the French Governor, Louis-Alexandre Des Friches de Meneval, had little alternative but to surrender.

On taking possession of the fort Phips discovered that the French garrison troops had already looted the King's stores, and had hidden what they had taken. Enraged by this deception, Phips' forces spent tens days pillaging Port Royal, and the French outposts along the Bay of Fundy, before demolishing the fort.

An oath of allegiance to King William and Queen Mary was administered to some of the inhabitants, and a President and Council were appointed from among them to govern the captured port. The new Council was ordered to report periodically to the Governor of Massachusetts, but otherwise was left on its own. On May 21st all of the Massachusetts' soldiers re-embarked, and the fleet departed from Port Royal the next day with their plunder and prisoners – the French Governor, and the Port Royal garrison troops – on board.

The fleet arrived back in Boston harbour on May 30th.[19] Within days a committee was empowered, by the Governor and Council, to take steps to ensure that all plunder from the Acadia expedition was secured in a store house; and that all arms and ammunition issued to the soldiers was returned to the colonial government.[20] Orders were given to disband the several companies of soldiers employed in the Acadia expedition, and to convey the French prisoners to prison in Salem, where they were to be held pending further orders.[21]

Subsequently, the Governor and Council of the General Court of the Massachusetts Bay colony appointed a committee with instructions to divide and share the plunder: 50% to the colonial government; and 50% to be shared among the officers, soldiers, and seamen of the Acadia expedition. Or, if more convenient, the committee was to sell the plunder and divide the proceeds accordingly. All of the captured artillery and munitions, however, were to be retained by the government of Massachusetts, the General Court.

Thereafter, a second committee was established to decide whether some of the imprisoned French prisoners from the Port Royal garrison might be given their liberty to seek employment and board with local families, until such time as they could be transported back to France in a prisoner exchange.[22]

The Canada Expedition

Encouraged by the ease with which Port Royal had been captured, the Governor and Council of the General Court immediately began to prepare for the seaborne expedition against Quebec. Financing the expedition, however, was another matter. The Acadia Expedition had cost the colonial government £4,000 more than was gained through the government's share of the plunder, but the capture of Quebec appeared to be the only way to put an end to the frontier war.

At this time, it was reputedly costing the colony £500 per diem to maintain warships at sea to protect its fishing fleets and commercial vessels against French privateers, and to support its frontier garrisons and troops in the field to protect settlements from attacks by the French and Indian marauders. This necessity, in turn, had forced the levying of heavy taxes on the colonists.[23] The General Court, however, hoped that the plunder gained through capturing Quebec would pay for the Canada Expedition.

Six days after the return of Sir William Phips from Acadia, the Governor and Council, with Sir William Phips in attendance, voted to undertake, as expeditiously as possible, a seaborne assault on Quebec; and to inform the neighbouring colonies and provinces that the Massachusetts Bay colony would be expecting their assistance in that enterprise. To finance the expedition, the General Court turned to the public and merchant community of Boston.

To encourage Gentlemen, Merchants, or Others to subscribe to loans to outfit and undertake an expedition against the French and Indians in Canada, it was decreed that such individuals would not only be repaid in full from the public credit, but would also receive a share of the expected plunder.

Once all of the charges for hiring the ships, for paying the Officers, seamen and soldiers of the expedition, and for the cost of the stores and artillery were defrayed, then the remaining plunder would be divided. The first claim would be for the payment of the shares proportioned out to the Officers, sailors and soldiers who served in the Canada expedition; and the remainder of the plunder would be equally divided between the colony and the persons subscribing to the loans.[24]

The next day, a seven-man committee, of which Sir William Phips was a member, was appointed by the Governor and Council to organize the Canada Expedition. The Committee, or any five members thereof, were empowered to seize and impress suitable ships for the Canada expedition with all of their stores and equipment, and to fit them up for service.

They were further empowered to employ tradesmen, seamen, and any others that might be needed for the service, to provide the provisions and other supplies for the expedition, and to appoint or impress the men required, in various capacities, to carry out the enterprise.[25]

The Governor and Council of the General Court then proceeded to appoint the commander of the expedition. Although the commander was declared to be acting in their Majesties' Service, the appointment, commission, and instructions were ordered and issued exclusively on the authority of the General Court of the Massachusetts Bay colony.

On June 12th, Sir William Phips was appointed "General of the Forces" in his Majesties' Service, to command an expedition by sea against the French and Indians in Canada, and received his commission and instructions. Among them were orders to impress five warships, as well as "victuallers, Attenders and fire Ships", and to outfit them for service at sea in the Canada expedition. At the same time a proclamation was issued for volunteers to join Sir William Phips, in serving Their Majesties in the campaign against the French in Canada.[26]

It was further decreed by the General Court that all gentlemen, soldiers and seamen who wished to volunteer were to sign on with the appointed Muster Master of one of the existing militia regiments, and to list a place of residence so that they might be ready to rendezvous, completely armed, at a place and time to be assigned by the respective Muster Masters. To encourage volunteers, the pay scale and benefits for service in the Canada expedition were established by the General Court.

It was specified that all Officers and soldiers would be paid the same as the Officers and soldiers who were currently engaged in fighting the Indians on the frontier, and that the Sea Officers and seamen would be paid at the same rates as for the Acadian expedition. In addition, one half of the plunder taken from the French was to be shared among them, with the exception of the captured stores.

If anyone were killed, or lost on the expedition, his pay and share of the plunder would be paid to the widow and children or, if unmarried, to his nearest kin. Additional financial support was to be provided to anyone suffering a loss of limb, or wounded seriously enough to be disabled from physical labour, from out of the share of the plunder due the colony.[27]

Having taken steps earlier to authorize the impressment of privately-owned vessels needed for the Canada expedition, the Governor and Council now proceeded to impress the ships and to appoint captains to command the vessels.[28] Thereafter, a scale of payments was established to compensate the private owners for the hire of their requisitioned vessels, and to provide wages for the Captains and officers of the vessels sailing in the Canada expedition.

On July 5, 1690, the Governor and Council decreed that the owners of the ships and vessels impressed by the colonial government, would be paid a fee of seven shillings per ton for each month of service; and that the tonnage of each ship or vessel would be measured in a conventional manner, by a carpenters' rule divided by ninety-five. In addition, it was:

> *Ordered that Captaines wages for Ships about 200 Tuns shall be Seven pounds per Month, the Lieutenant or Master three pounds ten shillings per month, the chiefe Mate two pounds five shillings per Month, the second Mate two pounds per Month And that the Captaines wages of ships of a hundered Tuns and upwards unto 200 Tuns be six pounds per month, the Lieutenant or Master three pounds per month, the 2nd Mate two pounds per month, the Captains of all ships or vessels from Sixty tuns to 100 tuns their wages to be foure pounds per Month, the chiefe mate fifty shillings*

per Month, the second Mate 35s per Month.

> Captaines of all vessels from fivety tuns and under their wages per month shall be three pounds, the mate two pounds per month all other officers wages in each ship and vessell shall be proporionable, noe second mate to be allowed in and ship or vessell under sixty Tuns.[29]

In sum, once a vessel was requisitioned by the General Court for service in the Canada expedition, the vessel, its captain and officers, were considered to have been 'hired' by the colonial government. The ship owners were to be paid a monthly fee for the use of their vessel according to an established ship tonnage formula, and the captain and officers of the ship were paid a monthly wage based on their rank and the tonnage of the vessel on which they served. Ship hire payments and wages were to be paid by the government of the Colony of Massachusetts Bay for the period of time during which a particular ship was impressed into public service on the Canada Expedition.

Concerned about the shortage of gunpowder in the colony the Governor and Council empowered yet another committee to proceed, with the assistance of the constables and officers of the colonial government, to search for any powder that might be concealed in vessels or houses by private individuals, and to seize and secure whatever was found for their Majesties' service.[30]

In addition, an embargo was placed on the export of provisions and ammunition from the ports of Massachusetts without a special license from the Governor and Council. It was to be enforced by the customs officers of the Massachusetts ports and harbours, who were ordered to seize any vessel seeking to contravene the embargo and to confiscate the vessel, and its cargo, for the service of their Majesties.[31]

To arm a newly-built warship, the *John and Thomas*, guns were requisitioned from an unseaworthy vessel, and from among some of the guns defending the Castle fortification in Boston. The Captain of a sloop, who was being sent to Port Royal to secure pilots for the Canada expedition, was ordered to stop on his return at Fort Loyal in Maine to inspect the guns and remove any serviceable ordnance. A month earlier, Fort Loyal on Casco Bay had been destroyed by French and Indian raiders, and its heavy guns were spiked. If any remained serviceable, the General Court wanted them removed and installed in the new warship.[32]

While preparations were underway to muster, through impressment if need be, the soldiers and seamen, ships, munitions and supplies, required to carry out a seaborne assault against Quebec, the General Court prepared the commission which set forth Sir William Phips duties as General commanding the Canada expedition. The Commission, which was dated July 4, 1690, made it clear that Phips was commanding the Canada expedition under the authority of the Governor and Council, and/or the General Court fully assembled, of the Massachusetts Bay colony.

The Commission given to Sir William Phips was quite explicit. It stated that he was authorized to take under his care and conduct the land and sea forces raised for the Canada Expedition, and was to discharge his duty diligently in leading and ordering his inferior Officers and soldiers "to attack, take, fight, pursue, plunder, kill, and destroy" the common enemy, the French and Indians, by both land and sea. In so doing, he was charged with:

> *"Keeping Your Officers, Soldiers, and Seamen in Good Order Commanding them to Obey You as their General, According to the Rules, and Discipline of Warr, And Yourself to Observe, and Obey all such Orders, and Instructions as You shall receive from the Governour, and Council, or General Court of this Colony for their Majesties Service pursuant to the Trust reposed in You, ..."*[33]

On July 7th the Majors commanding the militia regiments of the colony were ordered to forward their list of volunteers to the General Court so that orders could be prepared for mustering the soldiers and filling out their ranks through impressment, if necessary. Each town was to be assigned a quota of troops to be raised, armed and outfitted for service, and if there were insufficient volunteers, the number was to be made up of men detached from town's existing militia units.

On the forming of new companies, the company nominated its officers, and in some companies the soldiers even elected their officers, whose names were then forwarded to the General Court for approbation. If approved, the officer's commission was issued by the General Court, or the Governor and Council acting in the name of the General Court.

The appointment of officers proceeded throughout July. In the interim, orders were issued for a levy of militia units to cover the shortfall of volunteers, and for the assembly of all the troops at Boston on July 29th for service in the Canada expedition.[34] A force of 2,300 soldiers was to be raised for the Canada expedition, but only 716 militiamen volunteered for the expedition.

To make up the shortfall foot soldiers had to be taken from the five regiments of militia of the colony; and warrants were issued by the commanding officer of the Massachusetts militia assigning each regiment a quota of about three hundred men to detach for the expedition. The number of men specified for detachment from each regiment was proportional to the muster strength of the regiment.

The impressed men were ordered to rendezvous at their muster stations on July 20th to await further orders, preparatory to marching to Boston. A mustering station was specified for the men of each regiment at either Roxbury, Charlestown, Cambridge, Salem, or Boston.[35]

While arrangements were being made for mustering the troops for the Canada expedition, a day of prayer and fasting was declared for July 10th. All labour was forbidden on the Fast Day, and the ministers and their assemblies were called upon by the General Court to pray for the success of the Protestant religion in the expedition against the French, for the conversion of their Indian enemies through the Gospel, for the sparing of the colony from a threatening smallpox epidemic, and for the blessing of Their Majesties William and Mary, Parliament, and the whole English nation.

Five Puritan ministers were appointed to serve in the Canada Expedition to conduct services of worship for the soldiers and seamen.[36] As preparations continued, the clergy responded by exhorting the people to support the expedition through appealing to the defence of Protestantism and the Churches of God, English patriotism, and loyalty to the Protestant Crown under Their Majesties William and Mary.

Volunteers were assured that they were fighting a defensive war for the welfare and survival of New England, which could only thrive if freed of French depredations; and that they were fully justified in making "a brisk Salley forth upon the French territories". As exclaimed by Cotton Mather in a sermon to the troops, "We are driven upon a purely Defensive War, which we may now make Justly Offensive to the first Aggressors in it".[37]

At the same time, the General Court issued an appeal to the colony of Rhode Island to raise their militia forces and ships of war to join the Massachusetts' fleet on its passage up the Atlantic coast to attack Canada. A new tax of two and a half Single Country rates was also levied upon each town to help defray the expenses of the Canada expedition; and orders were given that the French troops captured at Port Royal be impressed for service in the expedition and distributed throughout the fleet with two or three men assigned to each vessel.[38]

The Governor and Council expected to receive encouragement from the Crown for the planned military campaign against Canada, as well as the support traditionally furnished by the Crown in supplying arms and munitions for the colonial forces. However, whether or not a supporting word, and arms and munitions, were received from the Crown, the General Court was determined to proceed with the attack on Canada. Dire necessity dictated that it could not be otherwise.

The dispatch conveying the plan of attack, and the determination of the General Court to proceed with the great enterprise, exclusively with their own resources if need be, was forwarded on July 19th to the Secretary of State, the Earl of Shrewsbury, in London.

> *"Right Honourable,*
> *May it please you Lord pp.*
>
> *According to our Obligation of Duty and sincere affection to your Majesties Service, we have by sundry occasional Conveyances as well as by one express, formerly presented your Lord[ship] With an Account of the publick affaires of their Maj[esties] Colonys in New England, and especially in reference unto a bloody Warr begun and carrying on against their Majesties subjects and Interest in these parts by a combination of French and Indian Enemies, ...*
>
> *And it is the concurrent Opinion of the whole that notwithstanding the great charge and Trouble we have been at in raising and sending our men, provisions and other supplys to their Assistance and Relief, that we cannot secure and defend the Remote Plantations whilst the Enemy forage and live upon us at our dwellings and anoy us upon all Quarters by sending forth Partys, in the mean time being quiet at home; ...*

... upon consultation had, it is concluded to Raise an United Force within their Majesties severall Governments as far as Virginia, to attack them in their owne Country, and that the forces from the Western Colonys joyne with the 5 Nations of the Indians in friendship with us, to make their descent upon Canada from Albany, whilst at the same time we send by sea to attack them at Quebek;...

...preparations are accordingly makeing to the utmost of our Capacity with such Shipping as we have to set forth, expecting that we should before this time have received his Majestys Commands respecting that Affair, and supply of Arms and Ammunitions as we humbly supplicated in our last; but the season of the Year is so far spent that an Omission of a little time longer may loose the Opportunity for this summer, and the Enemy by their continual incursions may utterly waste our Remote Plantations before another season.

We are not unsensible of the Greatnesse and chargeablenesse of the Undertaking and Vast import thereof; nothing lesse than Necessity could have forced us thereto without their Majesties Gracious encouragement and supply of shipping. ...
...a special Service to their Majesties for the Preservation of their Interest, hoping for their Majesties favourable Acceptance of our sincere Intentions and Endeavours to promote their Honor and Interest and the safety of their subjects under our care. ....

Simon Bradstreet,
Govr. In the name of the Council
Boston, in New-England, July 19th 1690"[39]

To the Puritans, as expressed to the Crown by the General Court and set forth in other contemporary writings, the defence of the realm necessitated an attack on Canada in what was viewed as a purely defensive war. The frontiers of New England could not be successfully defended against Indian and French marauders engaging in guerrilla warfare. The massacres of settlers, destruction of hamlets, and devastation of the land, would continue unless an attackwere made on Canada to destroy the French colony or subject it to the English Crown.

The 'Jesuits' were believed to be inciting the Indians to attack the frontier settlements of Protestant New England, and it was known that the Wabanaki were being supplied with powder and ammunition by the French in Canada. Hence, Canada had to be conquered or destroyed. The very survival of the English colonies, the safety of the people, necessitated an expedition against Canada – "Salus Populi Suprema Lex [Esto]".[40]

Financial support for the Canada expedition was provided by the Boston merchants who subscribed individual loans, of up to £100, £200, and £300, in response to the General Court's proclamation that subscribers would receive a repayment of their loan, and a proportional share of the plunder on the return of the fleet from Canada.

By early August the General Court of the Massachusetts Bay Colony had managed to requisition and hire, as well as arm and outfit, a fleet of 32 ships at Boston with sufficient victuals for a campaign of three to four months. However, only four of the vessels were warships of 100 tons or more; the rest were but small armed merchantmen, mere brigantines, barks, and ketches.

Despite the best efforts of the General Court to requisition all of the spare gunpowder and ammunition in the colony, and to purchase gunpowder and munitions from neighbouring colonies, there was a severe shortage of both. The flagship of the fleet, the warship *Six Friends*, had but 15 barrels of gunpowder for her 44 guns, and it was estimated that there was no more than 70 barrels of gunpowder in the whole fleet.

During the first week of August, with no supply of gunpowder, arms and munitions having arrived from England, there was much public debate as to whether the fleet should sail or the enterprise be abandoned.[41] Four months had passed since Governor Bradstreet had forwarded his dispatch of March 29th on the sloop *Resolution* to the Earl of Shrewsbury in London requesting arms and ammunition be sent by the Crown in support of the projected Canada expedition.

The dispatch had been accompanied by a letter from the Deputy Governor of the General Court, Thomas Danforth, to Sir Henry Ashurst, dated April 1, 1690, that had elaborated on the specific needs of the expedition where gunpowder, arms and munitions were concerned. The Danforth letter had asked Their Majesties to order the sending out from the King's stores of four or five hundred barrels of gunpowder, with an appropriate amount of shot, and four or five thousand fusees. The letter also suggested that if Their Majesties would order a number of naval frigates to participate in the seaborne assault against Quebec, it would greatly facilitate the undertaking.[42]

As of the early days of August, no reply had been received from London, and time was pressing. The New England fleet was fully outfitted and assembled in Boston harbour, and the militia companies were marching on the town from their muster stations at Roxbury, Charlestown, Cambridge, and Salem.

Although sorely in need of the gunpowder, arms and munitions expected from England, Sir William Phips could wait no longer. Further delay was impossible. If the attack on Canada were to be carried out during the 1690 campaign season, and the seaborne assault on Quebec coordinated with the planned overland attack on Montreal, the fleet had to set sail as soon as possible.

On August 8th a total of 2,300 militia men from Massachusetts and Plymouth, together with fifty Indians from Plymouth, were mustered at Georges Island in Boston Harbour, and embarked the next day on the ships which were anchored at Nantucket (Hull) at the south end of Boston harbour.

General Sir William Phips and Lt. General John Walley visited the ships of the fleet and gave directions as to how many soldiers were to be assigned to each vessel. When the wind came up later in the day on August 9th, General Phips sailed from Boston harbour bound for Quebec with a fleet consisting of four warships, 28 lightly-armed merchant ships, and several tenders.[43]

The fleet was divided into three squadrons: the Admiral's squadron under Sir William Phips, which included the flagship *Six Friends* (44 guns) of Captain Gregory Sugar Sr., the *John and Thomas* (26 guns) of Captain Thomas Carter, and ten other ships; the Vice Admiral's squadron, led by the *Swan* of Captain Thomas Gilbert with nine more ships; and the Rear Admiral's squadron, led by the *America Merchant* of Captain Joseph Eldridge, with nine more ships. Included in the fleet were five ships from the colony of New York.[44]

While organizing the military expedition to attack Quebec from the sea, the General Court had been pre-occupied with defending the outlying plantations of the colony, protecting the New England coastal settlements, fishing fleets, and commercial shipping against French privateers, and in mustering militia units to defend the eastern frontier of New England in Maine.

The very survival of New England appeared to depend on the success of the Canada expedition in conquering New France, and bringing an end to the devastating attacks of the French and their Indian allies. Once the fleet set sail, New Englanders could only pray that divine Providence would bring the Canada Expedition to a successful conclusion.

1. Thomas Hutchinson, *The History of the Colony and Province of Massachusetts-bay*, ed. Lawrence Shaw Mayo (Cambridge: Massachusetts-Harvard University Press, 1936), pp. 335-337; Theodore B. Lewis jr., "Massachusetts and the Glorious Revolution" (Ph.D. dissertation, University of Wisconsin, 1967), pp. 269-278; and Richard R. Johnson, *John Nelson, Merchant Adventurer, A Life Between Empires*, (London: Oxford University Press, 1991), pp. 55-62. John Nelson, a leading Boston merchant, had extensive pre-war trade ties with Acadia. He played a critical role in convincing the General Court to authorize the Acadia expedition as a private undertaking.

2. "Bill for Volunteers against the French", January 4, 1689/90, and "Committee to Consult referring to an Expedition against Port Royal", January 10, 1689/90, in Robert Earle Moody & Richard Clive Simmons, eds., *The Glorious Revolution in Massachusetts, Selected Documents 1689-1692*, (Boston: The Colonial Society of Massachusetts, 1988), pp. 191-193.

3. "Committee's Report about the French Affairs", January 18, 1689/90, and "Proposals to Encourage an Expedition against the French at Port Royal", February 6, 1689/90, in Moody & Simmons, *Selected Documents*, pp. 194-196, and 205-206.

4. Johnson, *John Nelson*, pp. 59-61. The raids of the French and their Indian Allies on New York were in retaliation for Iroquois raids in the fall of 1689 on French settlements at La Chesnaye and Lachine, and the massacre of the settlers. The Iroquois were supplied with arms and ammunition through trading with New York. Hence the French decision to attack the English border settlements to cut off trade with the Iroquois and give the English settlers a taste of Indian warfare on the frontier. On the raid, see W.J. Eccles, *Canada Under Louis XIV* (Toronto: McClelland and Stewart, 1964), pp. 169-173; and Francis Parkman, *France and England in North America*, Vol. II (New York: The Library of America, 1983), pp. 154-160. Schenectady was attacked by a 120-man force comprising 24 French and 96 Christian Iroquois from Montreal.

5. "Order for Setting Forth an Expedition to Nova Scotia", March 14, 1690/91, "Order for Ten Rates", March 14, 1690, and "Committee for

the Shipping, Provisions, etc. on the Nova Scotia Expedition", March 15, 1690/91, in Moody & Simmons, *Selected Documents*, pp. 224-226.

6. "Committee for Setting Forth the Expedition to Nova Scotia", March 19, 1689/90, and "Power to the Committee for raising men on the expedition to Nova Scotia", March 22, 1689/90, in Moody & Simmons, *Selected Documents*, pp. 228, and 233-234.

7. "Encouragement to Volunteers against the French", March 21, 1689/90, in Moody & Simons, *Selected Documents*, pp. 231-232.

8. Emerson W. Baker and John G. Reid, *The New England Knight, Sir William Phips, 1651-1695* (Toronto: University of Toronto Press, 1998), pp. 3-27. In 1675 the General Court had placed an embargo on the sale of powder, arms, and shot, to the Indians, which resulted in a great deal of suffering for them during the following winter. With the approach of the next fall's hunting season, the Wabanaki attacked the Sheepscot settlements to secure powder and munitions. On the hardships imposed on the Indians by a scarcity of shot and gunpowder, see *ibid*, pp. 164-165.

9. Baker and Reid, *The New England Knight*, pp. 27-75. On the petition of Phips and Increase Mather of February 18, 1688/89, see *ibid*, pp. 72-74, and Richard R. Johnson, *Adjustment to Empire, The New England Colonies, 1675-1715* (New Brunswick, New Jersey: Rutgers University Press, 1981), p. 146.

10. At least three Boston merchants were considered as commanders for the Acadia expedition and two, who were appointed in turn, declined the command before Sir William Phips volunteered and received his commission. See Johnson, *John Nelson, Merchant Adventurer*, pp. 61-62.

11. General Court Minutes, March 22, 1690, in Moody & Simmons, *Selected Documents*, pp. 233-234.

12. Baker & Reid, *The New England Knight*, pp. 78-79.

13. Johnson, *John Nelson, Merchant Adventurer*, p. 64; and General Court Minutes, May 30, 1690, in Moody & Simmons, *Selected*

Documents, p. 243.

14. "Agreement to desire a meeting of Commissioners from the Several Governments to advise of the Affairs of the Warr", March 19, 1690, and Governor and Council, Colony of Massachusetts Bay, "To All unto whom these presents shall come Greetings", March 24, 1690, in Moody & Simmons, *Selected Documents*, pp. 227 & 236. The attack on Salmon Falls is described in Eccles, *Canada under Louis XIV, 1663-1701*, pp. 172-174; and Parkman, *France and England in North America*, pp. 161-167. Salmon Falls was attacked by a war party from Trois Rivières consisting of 24 French, 20 Abernakis (Wabanaki), and five Algonquins.

15. *The Andros Tracts, Being a Collection of Pamphlets and Official Papers*, Vol. III, with Notes by W.H. Whitmore (New York: Burt Franklin, 1874), pp. 46-47, "Massachusetts Government to the Earl of Shrewsbury", Boston, March 29, 1690. To the Puritans, the projected attacks on Port Royal and Canada were defensive operations, as they were the ones under attack.

16. "Committee for Setting forth the Expedition to Nova Scotia", 19 March 1690, "Constables to Impress Seamen", 15 April 1690, and General Court Minutes, 18 April 1690, in Moody & Simmons, *Selected Documents*, pp. 228, and 238. See also Baker & Reid, *The New England Knight*, pp. 159-160.

17. Baker & Reid, *The New England Knight*, p. 95; and Johnson, *Adjustment of Empire*, p. 194.

18. "Order for the Detachment of 160 men", May 14, 1690, in Moody & Simmons, *Selected Documents*, p. 239; and Walter K. Watkins, *Soldiers in the Expedition to Canada in 1690, and Grantees of the Canada Townships* (Boston: Printed by the Author, 1898), p. 76, citing General Court Minutes, May 20, 1690.

19. Canada, *Canadian Archives Report, 1912*, Sessional Paper No. 29b, Appendix E., pp. 54-63, "Journal of the Expedition under Sir William Phips against Port Royal, 1690". The names of the seven ships are listed therein, together with their Captains, and the names of the Officers of the Regiment of Foot that sailed with Phips. On the Port

Royal expedition see also Baker & Reid, *The New England Knight*, pp. 83-95.

20. General Court Minutes, June 2, 1690, in Moody & Simmons, *Selected Documents*, p. 245.

21. General Court Minutes, June 5, 1690, in Moody & Simmons, *Selected Documents*, p. 247.

22. General Court Minutes, June 6 and 14, 1690, in Moody & Simmons, *Selected Documents*, pp. 248 & 253.

23. Letter from Captain Nicholson, James City, Virginia, to the Lords of Trade and Plantations, November 4, 1690, in Canada, *Canadian Archives Report*, 1912, Sessional Paper No. 29b, Appendix G, pp. 75-77.

24. General Court Minutes, June 6, 1690, in Moody & Simmons, *Selected Documents*, p. 248.

25. General Court Minutes, June 7, 1690, in Moody & Simmons, *Selected Documents*, p. 249.

26. General Court Minutes, June 12, 14, and 21, 1690, in Moody & Simmons, *Selected Documents*, pp. 251-252, 255, and 258.

27. "Proposal for Volunteers to Canada", June 19, 1690, in Moody & Simmons, *Selected Documents*, pp. 255-256. When the head of a family enlisted provision was made also to provide relief for the family during his period of service. Up to 2 shillings per week was authorized to be issued on the credit of the soldier's pay from which it would be subsequently deducted (Minutes, July 15, 1690, *ibid*, p. 267)

28. General Court Minutes, June 14, 20, and 21, July 3, and August 1, 1690, in Moody & Simmons, *Selected Documents*, pp. 254, 257-258, 262, and 273.

29. General Court Minutes, July 5, 1690, in Moody & Simmons, *Selected Documents*, pp. 264-265.

30. General Court Minutes, June 14, 1690, in Moody & Simmons, *Selected Documents*, p. 254. Earlier, prior to the Acadia expedition, the General Court had tried to purchase fifty barrels of gunpowder, and more if available, from the Pennsylvania colony. (General Court Minutes, March 14, 1689/90, *ibid*, p. 223.)

31. General Court Minutes, June 14, 1690, in Moody & Simmons, *Selected Documents*, p. 254.

32. General Court Minutes, 26 June 1690, and 4 July 1690, in Moody & Simmons, *Selected Documents*, pp. 259 and 262, and June 14 and 20, pp. 254 and 257. Fort Loyal, a palisaded work with 8 cannon, was attacked by a war party of 50 French and 60 Abenakis (Wabenaki) from Quebec who were joined by over 400 Kennebec and Penobscot Wabenaki. Almost the whole garrison of one hundred men were killed, most in a massacre that followed on the surrender of the fort. On the raid, see Parkman, *France and England in North America*, pp. 168-170.

33. General Court Minutes, July 4, 1690, in Moody & Simmons, *Selected Documents*, pp. 262-263.

34. General Court Minutes, July 7, 15, 17, and August 1, 1690, in Moody & Simmons, *Selected Documents*, pp. 264, 270, and 272.

35. "Quota of Soldiers for the Canada Expedition", 18 July 1690, in Moody & Simmons, *Selected Documents*, p. 271. Earlier on June 5, 1690, the General Court had ordered 153 men to be raised in the Plymouth colony, as well as 50 Indians. In all cases, if sufficient men did not volunteer, the ablest and most fit were impressed to meet the recruitment quota (Watkins, *Soldiers in the Expedition*, pp. 76-77).

36. General Court Minutes, June 28, July 5 & 31, 1690, in Moody & Simmons, *Selected Documents*, pp. 261, 264, and 272. A further day of fasting and pray was subsequently ordered for August 28th (*ibid*, p. 274). Smallpox had already infected some of the troops marching towards Boston, and was present in Boston. See M.H. Thomas, ed., *The Diary of Samuel Sewall, Vol. I, 1674-1708* (New York: Farrar, Straus and Giroux, 1973), p. 262, 25 July 1690; and General Court Minutes, June 4, 1690, in Moody & Simmons, *Selected Documents*, p. 247.

37. Perry Miller, *The New England Mind, Colony to Province*, (Cambridge, Mass.: Harvard University Press, 1962), p. 160-161.

38. General Court Minutes, July 14 & 15, and August 1, 1690, in Moody & Simmons, *Selected Documents*, pp. 266- 267, and 273. The cost of keeping the French troops that were captured at Port Royal and imprisoned at Salem posed a problem for the General Court. Earlier, on June 19th, the Court had ordered that the prisoners who remained in captivity and had not been boarded out, were "to be removed unto Cambridge in Order to their being disposed of and employed by their own Consent so as they may be Comfortably provided for without charge to the Publick" *(ibid,* p. 255). Employing them in the Canada Expedition was but another effort to relieve the Court of the expense of maintaining the prisoners.

39. *Andros Tracts*, Vol. III, pp. 48-51, "Letter of Governor and Council to the Earl of Shrewsbury", Boston, July 19, 1690. See also Ernest Myrand, *Sir William Phips Devant Québec, Histoire d'un siege* (Quebec: Demers, 1893), pp. 130 and 131. On June 12th, the Lords of Trade had recommended that arms and munitions be forwarded by the Crown in response to Bradstreet's earlier request of March 29th. The shipment, however, did not arrive in Boston until January 1691 (Baker & Reid, *The New England Knight*, p. 96).

40. See for example, Anonymous, "Journal of the Expidition [sic] to Quebec", 3 January 1690/91, in John Wise, *Two Narratives of the Expedition against Quebec, A.D. 1690, Under Sir William Phips*, Samuel A. Green, ed., (Cambridge: John Wilson and Son, 1902), pp. 27-28. The Puritans went to great lengths to deny they were engaging in an offensive war, but this was a religious concern, not political or constitutional. They adhered to the Christian concept of a 'just war', in which a resort to arms could be justified in resisting an aggressor. Oddly enough for a covenanted people governed by God`s law, the ultimate argument set forth to justify an attack on Canada was that of necessity, the survival of the people being cited as the supreme law: "Salus Populi Suprema Lex Esto".

41. Letter of James Lloyd, merchant, Boston, January 8, 1690/91, in Canada, *Canadian Archives Report, 1912,* Sessional Paper No. 29b, Appendix E, p. 65.

42. Hutchinson, *History of the Colony*, p. 337, quoting from a letter of Deputy Governor Danforth to Sir Henry Ashurst, April 1, 1690. During the summer of 1690, William III was heavily engaged in critical campaigns in both Ireland and Flanders in fighting against the armies of Louis XIV of France. Presumably, the Crown could spare little by way of supplying gunpowder and shot to the colonies at that time.

43. M. H. Thomas, ed., *The Diary of Samuel Sewall*, Vol. I, p. 263, entry for Friday, August 8 and Saturday August 9, 1690; and Hutchinson, *History of Colony*, pp. 337-338. See also Baker and Reid, *The New England Knight*, p. 179.

44. Anonymous, "Journal of the Expidition [sic] to Quebec", Boston, January 3, [1691], in John Wise, *Two Narratives of the Expedition against Quebec*, pp. 29-30. This is the most complete listing of the vessels in Phips' fleet. All of the Captains are identified, and all but two of the 32 ships are named.

Phips' Amphibious Assault on Canada – 1690

CHAPTER TWO

The Attack and Aftermath

On August 9th, 1690, a New England fleet under the command of Sir William Phips sailed from Boston Harbour to attack and subdue the French in Canada. The seaborne expedition was part of a two-pronged invasion strategy which sought to coordinate an overland attack on Montreal from New York with an amphibious assault on Quebec by sea from New England.

It was an audacious plan, born of desperation, and one which resulted in an abortive land campaign, a demoralizing defeat for the forces attacking Quebec by sea, and an unmitigated disaster for the New England soldiers and sailors of the Canada Expedition. Horrendous suffering from disease and malnutrition was experienced on the return voyage to New England, while the men struggled against Atlantic storms, contrary winds, and the terrible freezing cold of winter on the open waters of the Atlantic Ocean.

Chapter Two comments on the abortive overland attack on Montreal, and examines in depth the conduct of the Canada expedition: the voyage to Quebec; the failure of the amphibious assault on Quebec; and the cruel aftermath of the return voyage; as well as the heavy cost paid by the Massachusetts Bay Colony for the failed expedition.

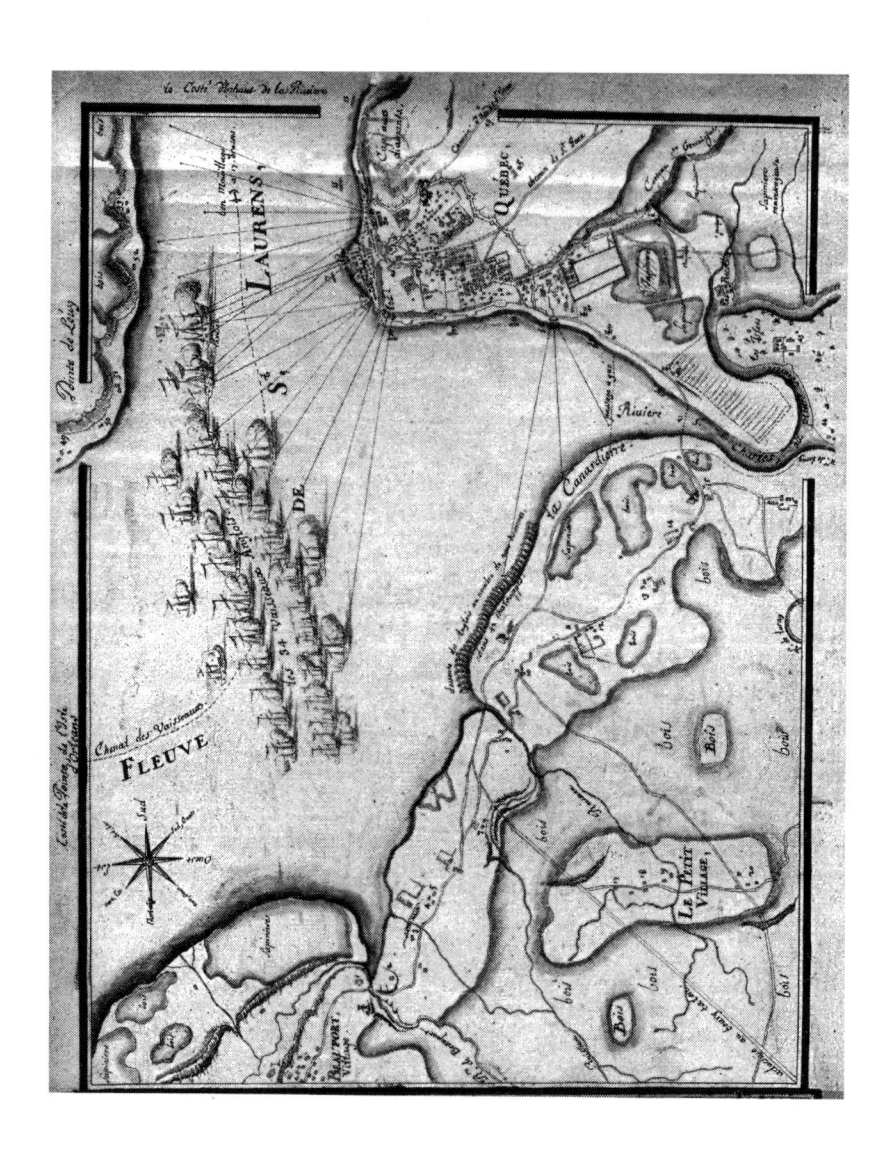

Map Two

Quebec under siege by New Englanders, October 1690. (Tracing: Harvard Map Collection.)

Chapter Two

The Attack and Aftermath

For over two years prior to the launching of the Canada expedition of 1690 the New England colonies had been at war in coming under attack first by the Wabanaki Indians on their eastern frontier, and then by the French and their Indian allies who attacked the northern frontier settlements. As the war progressed, the English colonies suffered widespread devastation on their eastern and northern frontiers, and the General Court of the Massachusetts Bay colony found itself in a desperate situation, fighting "an afflictive, distressing and bloody war".

It was seen as a war for survival. The General Court government of the Massachusetts Bay colony believed that the French aimed to destroy the English colonies as a prelude to conquering them, and extirpating the Protestant religion from North America. Only the conquest of Canada would bring an end to the French threat and bring security and peace to New England.

Under Attack

Efforts to defend the frontiers of the colonies had to be proved exceedingly expensive, and far from effective owing to the wide dispersion of the English settlements and the mode of 'skulking' warfare employed by the Indians. Rather than engaging in pitched battles, the Indians sent into the field highly mobile war parties that lived off the land and struck unexpectedly against isolated settlements, killing and carrying off the inhabitants and burning their farmsteads.

What was equally galling, the French attacking forces had adopted the Indian mode of guerrilla warfare, in living off the land and attacking by stealth. Raiding parties had penetrated within 30 miles of Boston, and a number of frontier forts and towns had been taken and destroyed, resulting in over 1,000 persons being killed or captured throughout the colonies.

On the eastern frontier, Maine was totally devastated and depopulated as settlers abandoned their farmsteads and fled in terror from the interior to Portsmouth. Both Fort Loyal, on Casco Bay, and the port town of Pemaquid had been captured and destroyed by the French and their Indian allies with over 200 killed.[1] And on the seacoast, French warships and privateers were harassing the New England fishing fleet, seizing vessels, and disrupting shipping, and in early July 1690, as the General Court assembled the Canada Expedition ships, word arrived that a party of French raiders had landed at Cape Cod.[2]

Pressed on all sides, the General Court was acutely concerned that Albany, on the New York frontier, was highly vulnerable to attack by the French. Albany was the key supply and communications centre linking the English colonies with their Iroquois allies. Should Albany fall to the French, it was feared that the Iroquois might well abandon their English alliance and go over to the French, thereby placing the very existence of the English colonies in jeopardy.[3] Hence the General Court had speedily dispatched 160 Massachusetts and 60 Plymouth militiamen to strengthen the defences of Albany in May 1690.[4]

In addition to deploying militia units to defend the Massachusetts Bay Colony from attack, the General Court during the summer of 1689 had to maintain upwards of 700 militiamen, including mounted troopers, posted in garrisons and on patrol duties in Maine.[5] Thereafter, in June, July and August 1690, a total of 600 militiamen were detached from eight Massachusetts' regiments by order of the General Court, and sent eastwards to support offensive operations against the marauding Indians in Maine.[6]

In July the General Court had also ordered two warships of the fleet, which were being outfitted for the Canada Expedition – the *Six Friends* and the *Swan* – to cruise the waters off Cape Cod to intercept and destroy the French raiders who were effecting landings on the coast.[7]

A Coordinated Attack by Land and Sea

During the months of June and July 1690, the General Court was busy in assembling, arming, and provisioning the ships required for the seaborne assault against Quebec, and in ordering the issuing of warrants for mustering the Massachusetts and Plymouth militia units required for that service. At the same time, New York and Connecticut were raising militia units for the planned overland assault on Montreal.

All three colonies, Massachusetts, New York and Connecticut, realized that the success of the projected conquest of Canada would depend to a large extent on a coordinated two-pronged attack, to divide the French forces through simultaneously attacking Montreal by land and Quebec by sea.

Over 600 militiamen from Connecticut and New York were assembled at Albany under the command of Colonel Fitz-John Winthrop of Connecticut, and by mid-July the militiamen proceeded northward towards Montreal to meet up with a force of 1500 Iroquois, who were committed to joining the expedition.

Almost immediately the overland expedition ran into serious problems. On arriving at Lake Champlain, it was found that the government of New York had failed to provide sufficient canoes and provisions for the expedition, and more canoes could not be constructed. The birch trees had already been stripped of their bark, and at that time of year the elm tree bark would not peel. Moreover, on smallpox breaking out among the militia, most of the Iroquois rapidly withdrew, or refused to join the expedition, rather than risk infection and exposure of their people to the potential devastation of a smallpox epidemic.

Quarrels broke out among the militia commanders concerning whether or not to abandon the attack on Canada. Finding it impossible to advance as a unified military force, both the Connecticut and New York militia units withdrew back to Albany. Only a small raiding party of 29 Albany militia and 120

Iroquois under the command of Captain John Schuyler pressed forward. On September 4, 1690, the Schuyler party attacked French settlements south of Montreal at Laprairie. Caught by surprise, over fifty settlers and French regular troops engaged in the harvest were killed, a number of farms were burned, and cattle butchered, before the raiding party withdrew to return to Albany.[8]

Unaware of the total failure of the planned overland attack on Montreal, the fleet of Sir William Phips departed from Boston Harbour on August 9, 1690, and continued to sail onwards towards Quebec. After a long voyage and delays caused by contrary winds, the Phips' fleet arrived at Tadoussac in the lower St. Lawrence River on September 23rd, and a Council of War was held on board the flagship *Six Friends*.

Articles of War were circulated to each ship, and copies issued to the officer commanding each company of militia. The 23 articles of war set forth the laws and ordnances that would govern the conduct and discipline of the soldiers, sailors, and ships during the pending battle, and the treatment of prisoners, women and children, and enemy property, as well as the seizure of plunder.

The first article clearly established that the New England fleet and soldiers were acting under the authority of the government of the Massachusetts Bay colony, and were subject only to the laws and ordinances of that government.

> *"Order: 1. That the laws and ordinances of war passed by the General Court of the Massachusetts, for the better regulating their forces; together with all such additional laws and orders as shall now be made and ordained by this Council at their present session; be forthwith read and published at the head of each regiment or company of souldiers, and on board each and every ship and vessel in their Majesties Service for this present expedition to Canada, etc. And that the*

same be put in execution according to the true intend and meaning thereof." [9]

Time was of the essence if Quebec were to be taken in a surprise attack but, to the dismay of the New Englanders, the Hand of Providence did not safeguard their enterprise. Indeed, the 'Hand of God' appeared to act against them. Almost a month earlier on August 29th, Phips' fleet had advanced past the Gaspé Peninsula into the estuary of the St. Lawrence River opposite Anticosti Island, only to be driven back and dispersed by strong gales and adverse winds with the resultant loss of several week's sailing time before re-entering the St. Lawrence River and sailing upstream to re-assemble the fleet at Tadoussac.

Subsequently, the lack of a pilot and continuing contrary winds slowed the fleet's advance against a strong current in an unfamiliar and highly dangerous river strewn with submerged rocks and sandbanks. Overall, it took 13 days to proceed 120 miles up the St. Lawrence River from Tadoussac to Quebec in covering what would have been a maximum of three-day's sailing distance on open water with favourable winds.

Despite a remarkable feat of seamanship in sounding the river and bringing a fleet of over thirty ships up a treacherous river without a single loss, the fleet did not drop anchor opposite Quebec until the early morning of October 6th.[10] The same day, Sir William Phips issued an ultimatum, under a white flag, demanding that Quebec surrender or be taken by force of arms.[11]

The Attack on Quebec

By October 6th, whatever chance the New Englanders had of taking Quebec by surprise had been lost. Almost three months earlier Governor Frontenac, on hearing that the English colonies were assembling a force at Albany to attack Montreal, had proceeded there with the French regular troops and militia from Quebec. Fewer than 200 men, mostly fur traders, merchants, and gentlemen, were left to defend Quebec, which was but poorly fortified.

Had the New Englanders arrived several weeks earlier than they did, Quebec would have been forced to capitulate or face almost certain defeat and capture by assault. However, as soon as the English fleet was sighted at Tadoussac, the French began feverishly to strengthen the landward fortifications of Quebec. Trenches were dug and palisades erected to the rear of the town, and guns mounted at points vulnerable to attack in taking advantage of the slow advance of the English fleet.

When informed by the Indians that the English land force had retreated back to Albany, Governor Frontenac immediately ordered all of the French regular troops and the militia units from Montreal and Trois Rivières to rendezvous at Quebec. Unbeknownst to the New Englanders, Frontenac had arrived at Quebec from Montreal on October 4th with 200 to 300 men, and the next day over 2,000 French regulars and militia marched into the town, followed by another 300 to 400 militia on the following day.

As of October 6th Frontenac had almost 2,700 men, both regular French troops and colonial militia units, assembled within the fortifications of Quebec, with additional militia on the Île d'Orléans.[12] Phips had but 1,300 militia men available for an assault on the town owing to smallpox having broken out on board ship, incapacitating a large number of soldiers.[13] The New Englanders' grand strategy – of dividing the French forces through attacking Montreal by land to pin down French troops, while a seaborne assault carried Quebec by surprise – had failed.

With the coming onset of cold winter weather, the New England forces had but two, or at most three weeks, to gain the city by assault before the river would freeze and trap their ships in the ice. With superior forces, Frontenac had only to wait with the Quebec fortifications to resist any attempted assault.[14]

Faced with Phips' surrender ultimatum, and confident of his

The Attack and Aftermath

superior military position, Frontenac gave a rather pompous reply. He denounced the Prince of Orange (King William III) as a usurper, and declared:

> "... je n'ai point de réponse à faire à votre général, que par la bouche de mes canons et à coups de fusil;...."[15]

In the interim, the New Englanders held a Council of War and developed a plan of attack. The main force under Lt. General Walley would be landed on the north shore of the St. Lawrence River in the morning, with the ships approaching shore and launching their longboats on the incoming tide. The landing site selected was the flats of the Beauport shore about two miles east of Quebec, on the far side of the St. Charles River.

Once landed, the men were to march to the St. Charles River where the smaller armed merchant ships would sail into the estuary of the river on the incoming evening tide, or during the night on the early morning tide, to land ammunition, provisions, and spades for the assaulting force. The long boats, propelled by oars, were then to transport the troops across the St. Charles River, with the armed merchant ships providing a covering fire during the crossing. Once across, field pieces were to be landed on the Quebec side of the river in order to provide artillery support for the troops in assaulting Quebec from the north east, and in breaking through the defences.

On the troops crossing the river, the four warships were to weigh anchor and commence a bombardment of the town. Once the attacking force gained entry to Quebec, and fired a building to signal their success, then the warships were to land a force of 200 men under the protection of their great guns, to make a direct assault, and force an entry into the lower town on the St. Lawrence River shore. To draw off French forces, several of the larger armed merchant ships were also to proceed up river to feign a landing in force above the town to the West.

On October 6th, the tides were not right to launch a landing following the receipt of Frontenac's answer to the surrender ultimatum. The next morning, an attempted landing on the incoming tide was thwarted when a sudden storm, with offshore winds, drove back the landing boats and prevented a landing.

One vessel, a bark transporting 60 men under the command of Captain Ephraim Savage, ran aground on shoals in the river and was stranded on the tide going out. During the day the fleet watched helplessly as the Canadien militia on shore exchanged musket fire with the soldiers in the stranded vessel, who appeared doomed when the French brought up two artillery pieces. However, Phips' flagship, the *Six Friends*, managed to manoeuvre close enough to shore, in the face of the storm and contrary winds, to fire several salvos with his big guns into the French force, which immediately retreated. On the tide coming in, the bark floated free and the men were saved.[16]

After having endured two days of frustration, on October 8th over 1200 New Englanders were landed from the longboats, and waded ashore at the Beauport flats in water up to their waists. The landing force came under fire almost immediately from a 600-man force of Canadien militia, French skirmishers, and their Huron Indian allies, hidden in the bushes, swamps, and thickets, along the shore. The landing, however, proceeded quickly.

Lt. General Walley's men charged forward, drove off the main body of the French skirmishing force, and established a bridgehead on the heights above the tidal flats. Fighting continued for over an hour until the last of the skirmishers were dislodged from a nearby barn, which was then put to the torch.

Only light casualties were suffered by the landing force, with four or five men killed, and some 60 officers and soldiers wounded, during the fierce exchanges of gunfire as the troops stormed ashore.

The Attack and Aftermath

On the retreat of the French force, the New Englanders dispersed to build fires to dry out their clothes, as confusion reigned on the beach. When advance scouts returned in the afternoon and reported that the St. Charles River (then at low tide), was shallow, and could be readily forded by the troops, one of the Puritan ministers, John Wise, berated Lt. General Walley for his inaction, and prevailed upon him to order an immediate advance to the St. Charles River.

The army was placed in battle order and began to march towards the river with drums beating and flags waving. The French skirmishers and Canadien militia, however, continued to harass the advancing force from ambush in the thickets and swamps along the roadway. As such, they adopted the guerrilla warfare tactics of the Indians in fighting from concealment, and ignored the taunts of the New Englanders to come out and fight in the open.

Almost immediately, the New Englanders plan of attack miscarried. On witnessing the intense fighting on shore, the torching of the barn, and the army marching in battle formation towards Quebec, the four warships weighed anchor and sailed upriver. At about four o'clock they began a cannonading of the town.

On shore, Lt. General Walley was urged by some his officers to push forward quickly to ford the river and launch an immediate assault on Quebec. Walley, however, refused. He ordered his men to camp by a small creek about 1/4 mile from the St. Charles River where shelter was available in a house, barn, and several outbuildings. He then proceeded, with one-third of his force, to the east bank of the river, but declined to cross. The advance force encamped on the riverbank to await the landing of provisions and munitions on the incoming evening tide.

With his militia companies short of gunpowder and ammunition, Lt. General Walley was determined to adhere to the original plan. He would wait until he had procured the needed munitions and supplies before attempting to ford the St. Charles River to establish a bridgehead on the Quebec side. Then the field artillery pieces needed for the assault could be landed on the high tide, and an assault on the town launched with the close support of the guns of the armed merchant vessels, which were to come close inshore on the rising tide. While Walley's advance force set up camp on the far bank of the St. Charles River across from Quebec, the naval bombardment of the town continued throughout the evening.[17]

In refusing to heed the advice of several of his officers to immediately ford the St. Charles River at low tide to establish a bridgehead, Lt. General Walley increased immeasurably the transport and logistics difficulties that the New Englanders faced.

Following the landing of munitions and supplies on the far side of the St. Charles River, the attacking force would have to be rowed across the river at high tide while the armed merchant ships moved into the estuary of the river to land the field artillery pieces and provide close fire support for the assault on the town. This involved a complicated series of amphibious operations that would have had to be coordinated to launch an attack in force; and that would have to be carried out under cannon fire from the fortress of Quebec.

From a logistical and operational standpoint, it would have been far better had Lt. General Walley immediately crossed the St. Charles River at low tide to establish a defensible bridgehead. Then the supplies, munitions, and field artillery pieces could have been landed directly on the Quebec side of the St. Charles River on the incoming tide, during the night under the cover of darkness. In the morning the armed merchant ships could then have come in on the rising tide to provide covering fire with their guns for an assault on the town at daybreak. It would have been a bold and daring thrust with a great prospect of success against a lightly-defended Quebec, but that was not the situation.

The Attack and Aftermath

Although Lt. General Walley did not know it, Quebec was heavily defended, and any immediate crossing of the St. Charles River, with his men short of gunpowder and munitions, might well have ended in disaster.

The French strategy was to let Walley's force cross the river. Governor Frontenac had deployed French skirmishers and militia units to harass the advance of the New Englanders along the Beauport shore, but had no intention of opposing a river crossing. Once the New Englanders were across the river, with their retreat cut off at high tide, Frontenac intended to launch a major counter attack, a sortie in force, with his French regular troops to utterly defeat and capture the entire attacking force.[18]

The cautious approach adopted by Lt. General Walley – in wanting to reconnoitre the situation, and wait behind the St. Charles River barrier for munitions and supplies before crossing the river to launch an assault on Quebec – was a far wiser decision than he knew, in the situation in which the New Englanders found themselves.

At Quebec, low tide was at four o'clock in the morning and four o'clock in the afternoon, and the St. Charles River could be forded only at low tide, and in but two places. When the tide came in, the lower reach of the river would rise three feet per hour to a maximum height of 17 feet. In effect, the New Englanders would have several hours at most to ford the tidal estuary of the St. Charles River, and would have to do so at a particular time of day at one of two known crossing sites where they would be under a heavy enemy fire. Moreover, there would be no possibility of retreat once the tide turned.[19]

During the night of October 8th, the efforts of the armed merchant ships to move into the St. Charles River estuary were unsuccessful in the face of strong offshore winds. The long boats managed to land only a small quantity of powder and shot, and six fields guns, at the shore encampment. The landing of the field pieces, however, was premature. It imposed a further burden on the attacking force as the six field guns would have to be transported across the St. Charles River in any assault on the town.[20]

The next morning, at dawn, the four warships resumed their bombardment of the town, and Lt. General Walley again refused to order an assault on Quebec. He held firm to his decision despite the urging of several of his officers, and of the Reverend Wise, that he take advantage of the morning low tide. However, an immediate attack on Quebec would have had to be undertaken without the close fire support of the armed merchant ships, and with only the six field pieces available for providing artillery support once they were transported across the river. In addition, Lt. General Walley was reportedly despondent, owing to information conveyed by a French deserter during the night.

Walley had learned that the planned overland attack on Montreal had been aborted; that Count Frontenac was at Quebec with a force of almost 3,000 men, having left only 50 men at Montreal; and that the town was newly fortified on the northeast at the site of the planned assault.

The New Englanders were faced with the prospect of attacking a heavily armed, and entrenched force of French regular troops and militia, with a lightly-armed militia force of less than half the strength of the defenders. They also lacked heavy guns and extensive field artillery support, to bring to bear at the point of attack. Moreover, by noon the naval bombardment of the town ceased.

When the four warships returned to the fleet, it was learned that they had almost exhausted their limited supply of gunpowder, yet had managed to inflict but little damage on the Quebec fortifications. The heavy 24-pounder guns of the Quebec batteries, however, had severely pounded the New England warships, causing a great deal of damage to their hulls and rigging.

The Attack and Aftermath

Trapped in a desperate military situation on the Beauport shore, with but few provisions, his troops low on ammunition, wet, and suffering greatly from exposure to the freezing cold, and an outbreak of a debilitating fever and a recurrence of smallpox, the New Englanders remained on the defensive, inactive, on October 9th. During the night their misery was compounded as temperatures plummeted, and a thick ice, sufficient to hold a man's weight, formed over ponds and still waters. The flowing waters of the St. Charles River, however, remained open.

The next day, Lt. General Walley conferred with General Phips. Once on board the *Six Friends*, Walley recommended that the troops be withdrawn from onshore, and rested for several days, before attempting another assault elsewhere. Phips agreed, and that afternoon the New Englanders were drawn up in battle order on the east bank of the St. Charles River preparatory to marching back to the Beauport shore to re-embark.

On seeing the New Englanders assembling their troops, Frontenac marched three battalions of French regulars, over 1,000 men, out of the city to take up a defensive position to repel an attack, under the protection of a town battery of eight great guns sighted to fire upon any attempted fording of the river.

To the New Englanders, it was now clearly evident that any attack across the river would be very rash, if not disastrous, with ill-equipped militiamen attacking entrenched regular troops supported by heavy guns and with no prospect of retreat once the tide came in.

No sooner did the withdrawal commence than the New Englanders were fired upon by a force of 200 militia, whom Frontenac had ordered across the St. Charles River in the early morning in order to harass any English attempt to undertake an advance across the river on Quebec. Concealed in the thickets and swamps bordering the river, the Canadien militia fired on the New England forces as they withdrew from their bridgehead on St. Charles River back to the Beauport shore.

Several major skirmishes took place that inflicted a number of casualties on both sides, but failed to disrupt an orderly withdrawal of the New Englanders and their six field guns. At the Beauport shore, sentries were posted, and the New Englanders kept in battle order ready to fight off any attack. The French regular forces, however, did not advance out of their defensive positions at Quebec, and the Canadien militia was kept at a distance by skirmishers who were sent out into the bush to protect the flank of the New England force on its withdrawal.

On October 10th an effort was made to re-embark the troops just before dawn on the incoming tide, but disorder reigned on shore in the scramble to be first off. Lt. General Walley was forced to order the longboats away. After a day of fighting off French skirmishers, the troops were hurriedly re-embarked in good order after midnight in the early morning of October 11th, during a heavy rainfall on a dark night that obscured their movements from the French.

Boats were sent to retrieve the six field guns, but Walley, fearing a French attack, ordered that priority be given to evacuating the men. In the rush to get the men off the tidal flats, with the tide coming in, five of the six field pieces became submerged in the rising waters and were left behind to fall into the hands of the French.

On October 12th prayers were held on board ship to seek God's guidance, and a Council of War was called by the New Englanders to re-assess their situation. The major issue to be resolved was whether to attempt a direct assault on the town under the cover of the great guns of the warships, or a landing on the Île d'Orléans to secure provisions for a landing to outflank Quebec and undertake a siege of the city from the north.

The situation did not look promising. Many of the men were reportedly sick and unfit for service, there was little powder and ammunition left for the soldiers' muskets, or gunpowder for the guns of the warships. Moreover, before the Council of War could meet a violent winter storm buffeted the fleet. The storm lasted four days, bringing exceedingly cold weather, strong freezing winds, and snow squalls.

Faced with an increasingly hopeless situation, Phips' fleet withdrew downstream opposite the Île d'Orléans.[21] On October 16th, a prisoner exchange was held with the French on the Île d'Orléans, and Phips' men began repairing the battered warships – mending damaged rigging, reinforcing splintered masts, and closing up shot holes in the hulls. Two days later, under a separate truce, the New England fleet purchased victuals from the inhabitants of the Îe d'Orléans, and then weighed anchor and proceeded down river.[22]

At Tadoussac, three French supply ships were sighted anchored upstream in the Saguenay River. The French ships – which were carrying flour, bacon fat (for making soap and candles), munitions, and a royal chest containing 200,000 livres for the support of the colony – had taken refuge in the Saguenay on being warned that an English fleet was descending the St. Lawrence River from Quebec.

Phips' warships attempted to enter the Saguenay immediately, but the wind shifted abruptly, making it impossible to ascend against the current. Over a five-day period, four attempts were made to ascend the river against contrary winds until a second severe winter storm, accompanied by a heavy snowfall, forced the warships to depart without seizing any plunder.

Adverse winds and the freezing temperatures of an unusually severe early winter, continued to plague the Phips' fleet as the New Englanders sought to gain the open waters of the Atlantic Ocean.[23]

Aftermath of the Quebec Attack

In Boston, unaware of the failure of the Canada expedition, the General Court took steps to provide for the men on their return. Warrants were issues for a new tax of Twenty Single Country rates; and a committee was empowered to secure a loan of £3,000 or £4,000 from prominent merchants and citizens to pay the soldiers and seamen and other pressing demands on the public credit. As security for the loan, the General Court pledged half of the new tax rates to be levied, the government's share of the plunder captured at Quebec, and all monies from the custom duties until the loans were repaid.

The committee was also ordered to confiscate all plunder from the expedition, to sell it at advantageous prices, and to submit an account to the General Court. Clearly the intention was to divide the plunder according to the decree of June 6, 1690, among the Officers, Seamen, and Soldiers of the expedition, the gentlemen, merchants and others who had subscribed loans in support of the Canada expedition, and the colonial government whose share was now pledged as security for new loan subscriptions.[24] Far more, however, would be required to deal with the aftermath of the Phips' expedition.

During the period from October 28th through October 31st fierce winter gales battered the New England fleet on its passage through the Gulf of St. Lawrence. Dispersed and isolated by the storm, many vessels were forced to find their own way home as best they could through unfamiliar waters, and once out in the Atlantic Ocean the remnants of the fleet were struck by winter storms that blew offshore.

Several ships were driven as far off course as the West Indies, while others experienced weeks of difficult sailing in combatting strong cross winds to gain the New England coast. Moreover both sailors and soldiers died in large numbers from smallpox, and a camp fever that had been introduced into the fleet by the survivors of the Beauport landing. Many also suffered greatly from the freezing cold and from hunger when the provisions taken on at the Île d'Orléans proved inadequate for such a prolonged return voyage.[25]

On November 7th and 8th, the arrival of several ships at Salem and Plymouth brought news of the total failure of the Canada Expedition. One of the first ships to arrive – the *Boston Merchant* of Captain William Shute – had lost 65 of its 120 men. The vessels arriving thereafter also had heavy losses with most, if not all, of the survivors on board reportedly suffering from a debilitating sickness.[26]

Sir William Phips arrived in Boston with the greater part of the fleet on November 19th, and both General Phips and Lt. General Walley immediately prepared reports on the Canada Expedition for submission to the General Court. Phips reported only 30 men killed in the fighting at Quebec.[27] As of December 8th, however, over 400 men were reputedly known dead, most of whom had died on the return voyage, and the fate of seven ships of the fleet remained unknown.[28]

By the close of the year, five ships were still missing, and it was feared that the death toll for the Canada Expedition would reach 1,000 men, in total, lost to the fighting, sickness, and shipwreck. What is more, the death rate soared among the survivors of the expedition. Weakened by their ordeal, many died in a smallpox epidemic that swept through Boston and environs on their return.[29]

The five lost ships were: a hospital ketch, the *Mary Ann* of Captain Gregory Sugar Jr.; a brigantine, the *Mary* of Captain John Rainsford; a bark, the *Elizabeth and Mary* of Captain Caleb Lamb;[30] a ketch, the *Hannah and Mary* of Captain Thomas Parker; and a brigantine, the *Adventure* of Captain William Bradlow.[31] Among the missing men were militia companies from Dorchester, Roxbury, Rowley, and Plymouth.

Early in the New Year the brigantine, *Adventure*, arrived in

Boston with the men of the Rowley Company. It was learned that Captain Bradlow's ship had rescued the men of the *Mary Ann* when that vessel had become shipwrecked; and that in mid-December the *Adventure* had been driven by severe cross-winds towards the West Indies. Arriving at Barbadoes in a semi-starved state, with a double compliment of men on board ship and all provisions exhausted, the men on the *Adventure* had had to sell their muskets and accoutrements to purchase provisions for the voyage back to Boston.[32]

The following spring, on May 9, 1691, Captain John Rainsford arrived in Boston, having sailed a small skiff with a five man crew on a daunting 46-day voyage from the Gulf of St. Lawrence. He and Samuel Gallop, the Captain of a Plymouth Colony militia company, reported that their ship, the brigantine *Mary* with 67 men on board, had been driven ashore on Anticosti Island during the fierce winter gale of October 28th.

Through building crude shelters and rationing provisions from the wrecked ship, the men had managed to endure the freezing cold of a northern winter, but with a heavy loss of life. On hearing what had happened, the General Court immediately dispatched a ship under Rainsford's command to rescue the men on Anticosti Island. Captain Rainsford arrived back in Boston on June 29th with but 17 men who had survived the winter ordeal.[33]

The fate of the remaining men of the Roxbury Company became know four years later when one member of the company, Samuel Newel, returned to Boston from Canada. Newel reported that his ship had been wrecked during a storm on an uninhabited sandy shore where some of the men drowned, others perished through starvation, and the remainder were either killed on encountering a party of Indians, or died subsequently in captivity. Only Newel survived. He had remained in captivity for a year, and then came into the possession of the French from whom he was ransomed after several years of imprisonment.[34] The fate of the Dorchester Company remained a mystery.[35]

On first receiving news of the total failure of the Canada Expedition and the condition of the returning soldiers, the General Court was appalled at the magnitude of the disaster. The colonial government faced the task of paying the seamen and sailors of the expedition, caring for the wounded, the sick and disabled, as well as the dependents of the soldiers and seamen who did not return. The public debt incurred in undertaking the Canada Expedition rose to £40,000 at a time when the colonial treasury was empty, with no prospect of further loans forthcoming from the merchant community and no plunder to divide up among the creditors and men of the expedition.[36]

The General Court, which had initiated and authorized the Canada Expedition, took full responsibility for the heavy costs of the venture on the return of Phips' fleet in mid-November. No appeal was made to the Crown for monies, nor was any claim made that the Crown was responsible in any way for defending the colony and/or paying the costs incurred. The General Court simply informed the King of the regrettable failure of the expedition, reiterated the necessity of undertaking it, and reported on the resultant distressed state of the colony in being exceptionally vulnerable to attack by the French and their Indian allies.

The colonial government requested only arms and munitions to defend the colony in keeping with the traditional support received from the Crown for the defence of the King's realm. The General Court did, however, ask that the King afford some assistance in defending the sea coast, the fishery and commercial navigation, which were vulnerable to French attack, and suggested that if the Crown would furnish frigates (and presumably financial and logistical support), New England would be willing to undertake a second assault on Quebec.[37]

Steps were taken immediately by the General Court to ensure that all public stores were returned to the government, and that all requisitioned vessels and guns and equipment requisitioned from other ships, were returned to their rightful owners.

At the same time, the General Court stated its intention to pay for all services rendered, and all debts incurred by the expedition. Payment could not be made immediately owing to the precarious financial state of the colonial finances, but the officers, soldiers, seamen, ship owners, and creditors were assured that they would be paid in full as soon as possible.

To that end, a committee was appointed to oversee the public credit, and on December 10th the General Court ordered the printing of paper bills of credit in denominations ranging from five shillings to £5. The bills were to be used for the immediate payment to all participants in the expedition, and government creditors who would accept the same. The Court ordered that no more than £7,000 in bills of credit be printed, and that the paper bills were to have the same face value as coinage.

It was also stated that the government treasury would accept the paper bills at par for the paying of all taxes and public levies, and would exchange the bills for money at their full face value when monies were available in the treasury to do so.[38] However, it was soon realized that the issue of paper currency was insufficient to pay the cost of the Canada expedition and for the maintenance of the garrisons defending the eastern frontier against attacks in the on-going war with the Wabanaki Indians.

On February 10, 1691, the General Court ordered the committee to print as many bills as were necessary to pay all soldiers and other claimants who presented debentures for monies owed for services rendered, and who would accept payment in the new paper currency.

To further encourage acceptance of the bills of credit, the Treasury was ordered to accept twenty shilling notes at a value of twenty-one shillings, and all other denominations proportionally in payment of taxes. Moreover, once again the public was assured that the bills would be redeemed by the government at face value in hard currency or in provisions of equal value whenever the Treasury was able to do so.[39]

To discharge the public debt and speed the redemption of the paper currency, the General Court immediately imposed yet another heavy tax, thereby adding to the already crushing tax burden borne by the Massachusetts Bay Colony.

An annual tax, designed to raise £8,000 per annum, was levied against the estates and persons of the colony for a period of four years with payments to be made in either hard currency, bills of credit issued by the General Court, or in grain at a money price set each year by the government. Individual tax assessments were to be paid by May 1st of each year, and when paying taxes in grain the taxpayer was responsible for defraying the cost of its transportation to government stores.[40]

With the unlimited issue of paper currency, the bills of credit soon depreciated by as much as a third of their face value, and many soldiers refused to accept the new currency in payment for their services.[41] The government responded by paying the soldiers in provisions and cattle received in payment of taxes, and carried through on its promise to accept the bills of credit in payment of taxes at the rates specified.[42]

As of May 1691, the issue of bills of credit was terminated at £40,000, the level of total indebtedness of the colony, and the printing plates were placed in safe custody by the government. By October 1691, over £10,000 in bills of credit would be taken in by the Treasury and burned.[43]

With the heavy taxes levied following the Canada Expedition, the tax burden imposed by the provisional government soared far beyond any previous wartime levy. As of the spring of 1691, a scant two years since the overthrow of the royal government of Sir Edmund Andros, the taxes that had been imposed totalled as much as the Massachusetts Bay colonists would normally have paid over a forty-year period.[44]

Over the winter of 1690-91 taxes climbed to thirty times the pre-war level as the General Court struggled to pay for the Canada Expedition, and to maintain over 400 troops in service on the eastern frontier in order to protect the colony against Indian attacks.[45]

Over the course of the summer, the General Court was forced to deal with recalcitrant towns and individuals who baulked at paying the heavy tax levies, and with town constables who refused or neglected to collect the several rates. Legislation was passed which empowered the General Court to impose heavy fines on constables who failed to collect the tax assessments in full, and granted the Governor-in-Council the right to appoint persons to collect the rates, if need be.

Moreover, the Treasurer was empowered to prosecute in the County Court of their shire all Select Men and Constables who were remiss in assessing or collecting taxes, with the Treasurer to retain one quarter of the fines imposed in payment for his efforts. Provisions were made, however, for the exercise of forbearance in enforcing fines or imposing jail terms on individual ratepayers who, in the judgement of the Select Men, might be legitimately unable to pay their taxes in full. Otherwise the General Court did everything possible to enforce the payment of the tax levies through fines and imprisonments.[46]

The financial burden on the colonists increased still further, in December 1691, when the General Court had to impose heavy duties on a wide range of imports and exports in order to maintain warships at sea to prevent French privateers from attacking the colony's commercial shipping and fisheries.

The customs duties levied far exceeded any customs duties imposed by the previous royal government of Sir Edmund Andros; yet any public discontent with the provisional government remained muted.[47] Many colonists remained traumatized from a fear of Indian attack, and from "the awful Frowne of God" upon them as evidenced in the abject failure of the Canada Enterprise, which overwhelmed every other consideration.[48]

For a brief period, in the early part of the year 1691, there had appeared to be grounds for hoping for relief from their trials and tribulations. In the eyes of the Puritan congregation the Salvation of God and His Divine Bounty were seen as acting to bring an end to some of the major calamities which were afflicting the colony.

The harvest of the fall of 1690 had been abundant; and by early February 1691 many of the sick were recovering from the smallpox and sickness epidemic that had swept Boston and the outlying towns on the return of the infected survivors of the Canada Expedition. The arrival of a supply fleet from England in the depths of a hard winter brought necessary supplies and manufactured goods, not the least of which was a plentiful supply of gunpowder and munitions for distribution among the town militias.

A truce, which was concluded with the Wabanaki, brought a temporary end to the fighting on the eastern frontier, and raised hopes – ultimately disappointed – that peace might be concluded with the Indians. And word spread that Divine Providence had bestowed glorious victories on the Protestant cause in Europe.

In Ireland during the previous summer, the new Protestant King of England, William III, had thoroughly defeated the deposed Catholic monarch, James II, and his Irish Catholics and French allies at the Battle of the Boyne, and, on the continent, the Roman Catholic powers had suffered a series of seemingly remarkable defeats.[49]

Equally encouraging, through the taxes levied -- at increasingly onerous levels -- the General Court was succeeding in paying down the public debts that had been incurred in the Canada Expedition and the Indian wars, and in providing monies for the care of the sick and wounded, and for the bereaved families who had lost a provider.

Individuals who had expended monies in caring for the sick and wounded on their return from the Canada Expedition, were reimbursed on submitting their claims to the General Court, and soldiers, who had suffered a debilitating wound or injury, were granted a small allowance or a pension depending on the severity of their disability.[50]

Arrangements were also made to ensure that the families of the soldiers and seamen who were lost during the Canada Expedition – most of whom were from the towns of Roxbury and Dorchester – would receive the wages owed for service by the deceased in the four-month campaign. However, deductions were made for any monies that had been advanced earlier to the families from the wages owed, and the wages paid to the families of individuals killed prior to completing the four-month period of service were reduced to accord with the actual length of service.[51]

During the summer of 1691 the General Court addressed the need to pay the owners of the ships that had been impressed for service in the Canada Expedition and had been lost.

Payment was to be made on the basis of the appraised value of each particular vessel as recorded before the fleet sailed from Boston the previous August. At that time, the General Court had appointed appraisers to establish the value of each ship of the fleet by way of establishing the government's level of financial liability if there was a need to compensate a ship owner subsequently for the loss of a vessel.

The General Court order made it clear that payment for the loss of a ship would preclude any further claim by the owners for payment for the hire of the ship during the Canada Expedition, and that anything removed from the vessels lost on the expedition would belong to the government.

The Attack and Aftermath

In effect, by paying the ship owner the appraised value of the lost or wrecked ship, the General Court purchased the property and established a clearly expressed right of ownership to the lost or wrecked vessel and its contents: viz. "And what is saved that did belong to any of the Said Vessels that were cast away in Said Expedition, to belong to the Country".[52] The compensation process, however, did not go smoothly.

The owners of all four of the lost vessels submitted petitions stating that the appraised value of their respective vessels was much less than the true value of their lost property. The owners of the ketch *Mary Ann*, and the brigantine *Mary*, received payment for the appraised value of their vessels, but their request for a re-evaluation of the appraised value of their vessels was refused by the General Court.[53] This was similarly the case with the owners of the ketch *Hannah and Mary*, who entered a series of petitions protesting that their vessel was worth more than its appraised value.[54]

The four owners of the bark *Elizabeth and Mary* – three Boston merchants, Nicholas Paige, John Pole, and Daniel Allin, and Mary Lamb, the widow of the ship's late Captain Caleb Lamb – entered at least two petitions protesting that the £300 appraised value of their vessel was £200 less than its true value. Ultimately the General Court ordered the treasurer to pay the owners of the said ship £387 "in full satisfaction for the same".[55]

Ultimately, all of the debts incurred in financing the Canada expedition were paid off by the provisional government of the Massachusetts Bay Colony, but the tax burden was immense. What the General Court never questioned was that the provisional government of the Massachusetts Bay Colony was solely responsible for the Canada Expedition and its costs.

It was a New England enterprise, authorized, instigated and undertaken by the Massachusetts Bay Colony, and subject, in the Puritan mind, only to Divine Providence – the Hand of God directing events according to His will in testing the faith and resolve of His chosen people. Several years later in writing a biography of Phips -- *The Life of Sir William Phips* (1697) -- the Reverend Cotton Mather, in recounting the history of the Canada Expedition, could but conclude:

> *"Thus, by an evident Hand of Heaven, sending one unavoidable Disaster after another, as well-formed an Enterprize, as perhaps was ever made by the New-Englanders, most unhappily miscarried;...."*[56]

Conclusion:

Following the overthrow of the royal government of Sir Edmund Andros, in April 1689, the colonial government of the Massachusetts Bay Colony was solely responsible for the defence of the colony. The provisional government, the re-established General Court, acted solely on its own authority in undertaking the Acadia and Canada expeditions as part of a concerted campaign to defend the colony through conquering the French territories in North America.

The General Court appointed the officers to their commands, impressed the soldiers and sailors for service, requisitioned the ships and supplies required, secured the financing for the expeditions through the Boston merchant community, drew up the Articles of War that governed the conduct of the expeditions, and took full responsibility for dealing with its aftermath.

The Crown did not sanction, nor support, either expedition; and neither Royal Navy warships nor English troops participated. All of the soldiers were militiamen from the colonies, either volunteers or conscripts, under the command of officers appointed by the General Court and under its authority.

All of the ships that participated in the two expeditions were either requisitioned commercial vessels, or warships built and commissioned by the General Court of the Massachusetts Bay

The Attack and Aftermath

Colony for its coastal defence. Moreover, it was the provisional government of the colony that bore the entire cost of both expeditions and the sole responsibility for paying the soldiers and sailors, caring for the sick and wounded, establishing pensions for the disabled, as well as paying for the requisitioned supplies and for reimbursing the merchant ship owners for the hire or loss of their vessels.

The Massachusetts Bay Colony showed a remarkable military capability in mounting two large-scale amphibious military expeditions within the course of a single year. In only three months, the General Court financed, raised, armed, and equipped a fleet of seven vessels to transport an army of 736 soldiers over 350 nautical miles to capture Port Royal in Acadia, and in the following three months financed, organized, supplied and equipped, an even larger seaborne expedition – comprising a fleet of 32 vessels, their crews, and 2,300 militiamen – to sail over 1,100 nautical miles on the open sea and through uncharted river waters to attack Quebec, in the heart of New France.

Moreover, when that stupendous military effort ultimately failed disastrously, through the Canada Expedition suffering a series of calamities beyond human control, the colonial government managed to raise a very considerable amount of money, £40,000, to take care of the sick, wounded, and disabled, to pay the soldiers, sailors and ship owners, and to compensate the proprietors of the four lost vessels. In sum, although the campaign to conquer the French mainland territories in North America ultimately miscarried, it was decidedly an amazing achievement in the annals of colonial warfare.

The Attack and Aftermath

1. Hutchinson, *History of the Colony*, pp. 335-337; Eccles, *Canada under Louis XIV*, pp. 172-174; Captain Nicholson, James City, Virginia, to Lords to Trade, London, November 4, 1690, in Canada, *Canadian Archives Report, 1912*, Sessional Paper No. 29b, Appendix G, p. 75; and Address to His Majesty from the Governor and Council, December 10, 1690, in Moody & Simmons, *Selected Documents*, pp. 287-289. Among the major settlements destroyed were: Quochecho (Dover), New Hampshire (Spring 1689, 23 killed, 29 carried off); Pemaquid, Maine (August 1689, 200 settler killed in Kennebec region); Schenactady, New York (January 1690, 60 killed); Salmon Falls, New Hampshire (March 1690, 34 killed, 50 women and children carried off).

On the tactics of aboriginal warfare, see: Patrick M. Malone, *The Skulking Way of War: Technology and Tactics among the New England Indians* (Baltimore: John Hopkins University Press, 1991). These were not just border skirmishes. Any alliance of the aboriginal nations against New England, with French support, posed a very real strategic threat to the survival of New England as a viable colony. See: Emerson W. Baker and John G. Reid, "Amerindian Power in the Early Moderns Northeast: A Reappraisal", *William and Mary Quarterly*, vol. LXI, No. 1, January 2004, pp. 77-106.

The New Englanders adhered to a European mode of warfare whereby armies, or large forces, would meet in the open to do battle, and fire musket volleys en masse at close range, with the aim of totally defeating the enemy in a decisive battle. In contrast, the Indians were adapt at forest warfare tactics – what the Puritans referred to as a 'skulking form of warfare' – which was characterized by mobility, stealth, surprise, and shooting accuracy, with the fighting consisting of raiding parties, ambushes, and skirmishes, aimed at inflicting casualties on the enemy, capturing booty, and taking prisoners for ransom.

2. General Court minutes, January 10, 1689/90, and July 8 & 14, 1690, in Moody & Simmons, *Selected Documents*, pp. 192-193 & 265-266.

3. Eccles, *Canada Under Louis XIV*, pp. 176-177. In early 1689 Louis XIV had approved a plan for an army of 1,400 French soldiers and 600 militia to attack Albany from Canada, and join forces with French warships in a combined land and sea assault to conquer New York. All non-Roman Catholics were to be expelled from New York to the other English colonies following the conquest. The fighting in Europe, however, made it impossible for France to furnish the soldiers and warships required to implement the plan. See Gustave Lanctot, *A History of Canada, Vol. 2, From the Royal Régime to the Treaty of Utrecht, 1663-1713* (Toronto: Clarke, Irwin & Co., 1964), p. 114.

4. "Order for the Detachment of 160 men", May 14, 1690, in Moody & Simmons, *Selected Documents*, p. 194.

5. Deputy Governor Danforth, to Sir H. Ashurst, April 1, 1690, quoted in Hutchinson, *History of the Colony*, p. 337. To pay for military defence measures, the General Court had to levy heavy taxes on the colony that reportedly impoverished the people. The rates imposed to that date totalled £20,000 (*ibid*). The territory of Maine was governed by the General Court of Massachusetts to which the towns of Maine sent elected deputies, and would continue to do so until Maine became a separate state in 1820.

6. General Court Minutes, June 10, July 17, 25, and August 1, 1690, in Moody & Simmons, *Selected Documents*, pp. 250, 267, 269, and 273.

7. General Court Minutes, 14 July 1690, in Moody & Simmons, *Selected Documents*, p. 266.

8. Hutchinson, *History of the Colony*, p.338; James Lloyd, merchant, Boston, January 8, 1690/91, in Canada, *Canadian Archives Report, 1912*, Sessional Paper No. 29b, Appendix E, p. 64; Captain Nicholson, James City, Virginia, to the Lords of Trade, November 4, 1690, *ibid*, Appendix G, p. 76; and Eccles, *Canada Under Louis XIV*, p. 179. See also, Francis Parkman, *Count Frontenac and New France under Louis XIV* (Toronto: George N. Morang & Co., 1899), pp. 268-270. The Massachusetts soldiers dispatched to Albany were posted to garrison duty in the frontier posts.

Smallpox was a highly infectious disease that struck the North American colonies in periodic waves of epidemics between 1660 and 1775. It struck almost everyone exposed to it, was extremely fatal, and could cause severe disfigurement. Among white settlers, the mortality rate was generally about 14%, but could range from 10% to as high as 50%; whereas among the Indians, who had no immunity from surviving previous epidemics, the death rate ranged from 55% to 90%. Colonists and Indians alike were terrified of smallpox, and had no defence against that disease in the 17th century.

Subsequently, inoculation (or variolation), introduced to Boston from England in 1721, proved somewhat effective in abating the death rate. It was superseded after 1796 by vaccination, the efficacy of which was proven by Edward Jenner in England. See John Duffy, *Epidemics in Colonial America* (Port Washington, N.Y.: Kennikat Press, 1972), Chapter 11, "Smallpox", pp. 16-112.

9. Articles of War in "Major Walley's Journal in the Expedition against Canada in 1692" [sic]. A Narrative of the Proceedings to Canada, so far as concerned the land army", November 27, 1690, reprinted in Watkins, *Soldiers in the Expedition to Canada in 1690*, pp. 7-9. Major Walley was the commander of a militia regiment; however, he was given the brevet rank of Lt. General when serving as the commander of the soldiers of the Phips' Canada Expedition.

10. Major Walley's Journal, November 27, 1690, in Watkins, *Soldiers in the Expedition*, p. 6; and Cotton Mather, *The Life of Sir William Phips*, Mark Van Doren, ed. (New York: AMS Press, 1919, 1st. ed. 1797), pp. 69-70 & 82. See also Anonymous, "Journal of the Expedition [sic] to Quebec', in *Two Narratives of the Expedition against Quebec*, pp. 31-34. The difficulties that sailing ships encountered in ascending the St. Lawrence River to Quebec, are well described in Gilles Proulx, *Between France and New France, Life Aboard the Tall Sailing Ships* (Toronto: Dundurn Press, 1984), p. 77-80.

11. Phips' ultimatum, reprinted in Mather, *The Life of Sir William Phips*, p.73.

12. "Relation de Sylvanus Davis", in Myrand, *1690, Phips Devant Québec*, p. 91; Eccles, *Canada Under Louis XIV*, p. 1890; and Parkman, *Count Frontenac*, pp. 270-271. In these chapters, the dates cited follow the Old Style Julian calendar which Britain and its colonies used until 1752. The French had already adopted the New Style Gregorian calendar, which differed by ten days in the late 17th century. Hence Phips arrived at Quebec on October 6th (Old Style), or in French accounts on October 17th (New Style).

In the Julian calendar, the New Year started on March 25th, rather than January 1st, and hence the practice by historians of citing the dates between January 1st and March 24th with a dual year reference, for example, January 1, 1690/91 through to March 24, 1690/91.

13. Major Walley's Journal, November 27, 1690, in Watkins, *Soldiers in the Expedition*, p. 11. See also Anonymous, "Expidition [sic] to Quebec", 3 January 1690/1, in *Two Narratives of the Expedition*, p. 37.

14. Eccles, *Canada Under Louis XIV*, pp. 180-181.

15. "Relation de Monseignat", in Myrand, *1690, Phips Devant Québec*, p. 27. Translation: "I have no reply to make to your general other than from the mouths of my cannon and muskets....."

16. Major Walley's Journal, November 27, 1690, pp. 10-11, of Watkins, *Soldiers in the Expedition*; and Mather, *Life of Sir William Phips*, pp. 76-77.

17. "Major Walley's Journal ", reprinted in Watkins, *Soldiers of the Expedition*, pp. 10-20; and letter, Major Thomas Savage, Boston, to Perez Savage, London, February 2, 1690/1, in Watkins, *ibid*, pp. 21-2. See also, "The Narrative of Mr. John Wise, Minister of God's Word at Chebacco", 23 December 1690, pp. 7-18, and Anonymous, "Journal of the Expidition [sic] to Quebec", January 3, 1690/1, in *Two Narratives of the expedition*, pp. 37-39.

18. Baker & Reid, *The New England Knight*, p. 98.

19. The analysis of the tides in October 1690 is from Eccles, *Canada Under Louis XIV*, p. 162.

20. "Major Walley's Journal", 27 November 1690, in Watkins, *Soldiers in the Expedition*, pp. 11-15; and Major Thomas Savage to Perez Savage, 5 February 1690/91 in Watkins, *ibid*, pp. 21-23. Afterwards, the Reverend Cotton Mather charged that "some believed that the Captains were afraid to risk their ships in going into the shallows of the estuary after what happened to the Bark" (Mather, *Life of Sir William Phips*, p. 78).

21. "Major Walley's Journal", in Watkins, *Soldiers in the Expedition*, pp. 10-20; and letter, Major Thomas Savage, Boston, to Perez Savage, London, February 2, 1690/91, in Watkins, *ibid*, pp. 21-22. See also Mather, *Life of Sir William Phips*, pp. 79-82; and "The Narrative of Mr. John Wise, Minister of God's Word at Chebacco", 23 December 1690, pp. 7-18, and Anonymous, "Journal of the Expidition [sic] to Quebec", January 3, 1690/91, pp. 37-39, in *Two Narratives of the expedition*.

The four warships, on returning from the bombardment of Quebec, had reportedly not enough gunpowder left to fire more than two rounds apiece. Lt. General Walley was accused of cowardice by the Reverend John Wise for not launching an assault on Quebec, despite the unpromising situation. Several testimonials, signed later by the gunners, also blamed Lt. General Walley for the abandonment of the five field pieces.

22. "Memoire pour 1690" in *Collection des Manuscrits contenant lettres, mémoires et autre documents historiques relatifs à la Nouvelle France*, Vol. I (Québec: A. Côté, 1883), pp. 576-577. On October 12th, just before the storm broke, the French had reinforced the Île d'Orléans with 200 men *(ibid*, p. 576). See also Francis Parkman, *Count Frontenac*, pp. 291-292.

23. Contemporary French accounts reprinted in Myrand, *1690, Phips Devant Québec*, pp. 49-50, 57-58, 77-78 & 91. The French supply ships waited two days before coming out of the Saguenay and then sailed quickly to Quebec on favourable winds. However, the French

ships did experience difficulty in docking, owing to ice conditions in the St. Lawrence River, by which time the St. Charles River was almost completely frozen over .

24. General Court Minutes, November 6, 1690, in Moody & Simmons, *Selected Documents*, pp. 283-284. A discount of one-third was given for making tax payments in cash, and citizens who were owed money by the government could receive payment in the form of a tax credit.

25. Mather, *Life of Sir William Phips*, p. 91; Hutchinson, *History of the Colony*, p. 340; and Samuel Myles, Minister, Boston, letter of December 12, 1690, in *Calendar of State Papers, Colonial Series: America and the West Indies, 1693-1696* (H.M. Stationery Office, 1903), Paper No. 1,239, p. 369. Some men had to have frozen toes amputated. See also Watkins, *Soldiers of the Expedition*, "List of Wounded", pp. 30-31.

26. *Diary of Samuel Sewall*, November 8, 1690, p. 269; James Lloyd, merchant, Boston, letter of January 8, 1691, in Canada, Canadian Archives Report, 1912, Sessional Paper No. 29b, Appendix E, p. 65; and Samuel Myles, Minister, Boston, December 12, 1690, in *Calendar of State Papers, Colonial Series, America and West Indies*, Paper No. 1239, p. 369. Among the dead, cast overboard during the return voyage, were many of the fifty Plymouth Indians who had no immunity to European diseases.

27. Hutchinson, *History of Massachusetts*, p. 339-340; "Major Walley's Journal", 27 November 1690, reprinted in Watkins, *Soldiers in the Expedition*, pp. 6-20; and Account of Sir William Phips, April 21, 1691, *Calendar of State Papers, America and West Indies*, Paper No. 1,417, p. 415.

28. Extract of a Letter, Boston, December 8, 1690, in *Calendar of State Papers, America and West Indies*, Paper No. 1,313, p. 385.

29. James Lloyd, merchant Boston, 8 January 1690/91, in Canada, *Sessional Papers of the Parliament of Canada*, 1912, Appendix E, pp. 65-66; Governor Henry Sloughter, New York, letter, May 6, 1691, quoted in Eccles, *Canada Under Louis XIV*, p. 184; and Joseph Dudley to William Blathwayt, February 5, 1690/91, *Calendar of State Papers,*

The Attack and Aftermath

America and West Indies, Paper No. 1,315, p. 387.

Lloyd speculated that at the rate survivors of the expedition were succumbing to smallpox, only one-quarter of them would be alive by the spring of 1691. A major smallpox epidemic raged in Canada and New England in 1689-90, and spread as far south as New York. It struck Boston particularly hard in June, July, and August, 1690, killing 320 persons. The ships, on returning from the Canada Expedition, brought a renewed smallpox contagion to Boston. See Duffy, *Epidemics in Colonial America*, p. 48.

30. Owners' Petitions to the General Court for the *Mary Ann*, and the *Mary*, 25 June 1691, in Moody & Simmons, *Selected Documents*, pp. 333; and Massachusetts Archives, Council Record, vol. 61, pp. 342-343, *Elizabeth and Mary* petition, n.d. The author is indebted to Dr. Emerson W. Baker, Associate Professor, Salem State College, Salem, Massachusetts, for furnishing photocopies of a number of unpublished archival documents from the Massachusetts Archives pertaining to the lost ships (cited hereafter as MA). Dr. Baker, a historical archaeologist and co-author, with John Reid, of a biography of Sir William Phips, *The New England Knight* (1998), was consulted by Parks Canada to help identify the shipwreck discovered in the St. Lawrence River in December 1994 near Baie Comeau, Quebec. It was identified as the *Elizabeth and Mary*.

31. MA, Council Record, vol. 37, p. 319, Petition of Edward Willy to the General Court, March 19, 1692; and Petition of Joseph Jewett Jr. to the Governor and Council, April 22, 1691, in Watkins, *Soldiers in the Expedition*, p. 54. See also Mather, *Life of Sir William Phips*, p. 91. In addition two ships were "cast away" during the return voyage; and yet another, the *Eagle Rose*, burnt on its arrival in Boston on December 1st. See Major Savage, Boston, to Brother, February 2, 1690/91, *Calendar of State Papers, America and West Indies*, Paper No. 1,314, p. 386; and Myrand, *1690, Phips Devant Québec*, p. 142.

32. MA, Council Record, vol. 37, p.49a, Deposition of Philip Nelson and David Benet of Rowley, April 25, 1691; and MA, Council Record, vol. 70, p.507, Petition of Thomas Jackson of Piscataqua, February 1699/1700. At least one man, Solomon Stuard, died of starvation aboard the *Adventure*. See also Myrand, *1690 Phips Devant Québec*,

p.161.

33. Mather, *Life of Sir William Phips*, pp. 92-103; Watkins, *Soldiers in the Expedition*, pp.80-81; and *Diary of Samuel Sewall*, June 29, 1691, p. 279. In Mather's account, there are thinly veiled hints of cannibalism, and a proffered justification for such given the dire circumstances of their winter's ordeal as related in detail by Mather.

34. MA, Council Record, vol. 70, p. 247, Petition of Samuel Newel of Roxbury, To the Governor & Counsel and Representatives Setting in Boston, June 5, 1695. Newel did not name the ship on which the Roxbury Company sailed, which is unfortunate as two ships remained lost and unaccounted for in the historical record: the *Elizabeth and Mary;* and the *Mary Ann*. He was voted £25 by the General Court for his military service and to compensate his family for the cost of his ransom from the French.

35. The small town of Dorchester and its surrounding area contributed 74 men to the Canada Expedition. In addition to the men lost with the sinking of the *Elizabeth and Mary*, apparently another 47 men who participated in the Canada Expedition died as a result: 33 of smallpox, and 24 of the fever. See William Dana Orcutt, *Good Old Dorchester, A Narrative History of the Town, 1630-1893* (Cambridge: Published by Author, 1893), pp. 90-92.

36. Baker & Reid, *The New England Knight*, p. 104. Various sources cite the £40,000 cost of the Canada expedition. See for example, H. Sloughter to Earl of Nottingham, May 6, 1691, in *New York Colonial Documents, Vol. III*, p. 761; and John Oldmixon, *The British Empire in America containing the history of the discovery, settlement, progress and present state of all the British Colonies on the continent and islands of America*, Vol. I. (London: J. Nicholson, B. Tooke, 1708, microform, 1969), p. 67.

37. "Humble Address of the Governor and Council and the General Court", December 10, 1690, in Moody & Simmons, *Selected Documents*, pp. 287-289; Governor and Council to Massachusetts Agents, 29 November 1690, *ibid*, pp. 411-415; and "To the Right Honourable, the Lords of the Committee for Trade and Foreign Plantations", [April 21, 1691], *ibid*, pp. 482-485.

The Attack and Aftermath

38. Order of the General Court, December 10, 1690, in Moody & Simmons, *Selected Documents*, p. 290. Apparently, these were the first bills of credit issued in an American colony.

39. Order of the General Court, February 6, 1690/91, in Moody & Simmons, *Selected Documents*, pp. 296-297.

40. Order of the General Court, February 10, 1690/91, in Moody & Simmons, *Selected Documents*, pp. 298-99. Among the taxes levied were: a tax of 6 rates in November 1689; 1.5 rates (to raise about £2,000) on December 4, 1689; ten country rates on March 14, 1690 (payable in corn, wheat, rye, oats, Indian corn, pease, barley, barley malt, and/or cattle, with a 1/3 reduction for payment in hard currency); 2.5 country rates on July 15, 1690; and twenty single country rates on November 6, 1690, several weeks before the return of the Phips' expedition.

41. William Pencak, *War, politics, and revolution in provincial Massachusetts*, (Boston: Northeastern University Press, 1981), p. 17; and R. Johnson, *Adjustment to Empire*, p. 198.

42. Order of the General Court, First Thursday in December, [1691], quoted in Myrand, *1690, Phips Devant Quebec*, p. 138.

43. Orders of the General Court, May 26, 1691, and October 24, 1691, in Moody & Simmons, *Selected Documents*, pp. 311-312, and p. 334. To wind up its outstanding debts, on April 17, 1691, the General Court ordered that anyone having a debenture for payment of services rendered should come forth within three months of that day to settle their accounts (presumably by accepting payment in bills of credit), or otherwise their claims would be excluded unless the individual were out of the country as of the date of the order (*ibid*, pp. 304-305).

44. David S. Lovejoy, *The Glorious Revolution in America* (New York: Harper & Row Publishers, 1972), pp. 350-351.

45. Pencak, *Wars, Politics, and revolution*, p. 17; and R. Johnson, *Adjustment to Empire*, p. 198.

46. "Watertown Petition", February 11, 1691, and Orders of the General Court, April 17, 1691, and 27 and 29 May 1691, in Moody & Simmons, *Selected Documents*, pp. 300-302, 306, 313, and 317-318. See also *ibid*, 16 March, 1690, p. 224, and Lovejoy, *The Glorious Revolution*, p. 350. The Select Men were responsible for apportioning the town's tax rate amongst its rate payers, for issuing the warrants for the constable to collect the taxes and for receiving the collected taxes for forwarding to the Treasurer of the General Court.

47. Order of the General Court, December 25, 1691, in Moody & Simmons, *Selected Documents*, p. 345; and R. Johnson, *Adjustment to Empire*, p. 199.

48. R. Johnson, *Adjustment to Empire*, pp. 202-206. The phrase quoted is from p. 206. The Puritans believed in Divine Providence: that it was the Hand of God that controlled events in keeping with His will. Hence, the Hand of God was seen as having defeated the Canada Expedition though sending smallpox, contrary winds, storms, and unseasonably cold weather, to thwart the New England forces; and the Canada Expedition disaster inflicted a strong psychological blow on the New England Puritans. However, ultimately it was interpreted as God testing the resolve of His chosen people to carry forward the struggle against the Catholics of New France with greater diligence and force in the future. See "The Narrative of Mr. John Wise, Minister of God's Word at Chebacco", in *Two Narratives of the Expedition*, pp. 5-18; and Mather, *The Life of Sir William Phips*, p. 82.

49. "A Thanksgiving Appointed", Order of the General Court, February 10, 1691, in Moody & Simmons, *Selected Documents*, pp. 297-298; and "Commissioners to Meet the Indians", April 14. 1691, in *ibid*, p. 303. In Europe, the spring of 1690 had been a bleak period for Protestantism. Louis XIV invaded and laid waste the Protestant Palatinate in Germany, and the deposed Catholic King James II landed in Ireland and proceeded to conquer much of the country with the support of French troops and Irish Catholic sympathizers. However, subsequently a Protestant army – comprising Dutch, English, and Danish troops – re-conquered most of the major Irish ports and cities, and fought the Battle of the Boyne on July 1st (July 12th, N.S.).

The Attack and Aftermath

At the Boyne, King William III personally inflicted a decisive defeat on a combined French and Irish-Catholic army and drove the French and James II out of Ireland. Elsewhere in Europe, an allied force inflicted a major defeat on the French army at Walcourt in the Spanish Netherlands. Hence, although the Canada Expedition proved a disaster, there were victories elsewhere in the summer of 1690 to relieve the New England Puritans of their immediate fears for the survival of Protestantism.

50. See for example Moody & Simmons, *Selected Documents*, pp. 129-130, Petition of Major Nath. Wade, October 17, 1691, p. 321, Order of the General Court, 2 June 1691, p. 335, Order to pay for disbursements on sick and wounded landed in Salem, October 24, 1691, and pp. 318-319, Stipends, May 30, 1691. Decades later, in a belated effort to more fully compensate the officers and soldiers of the Canada expedition, the General Court in 1735 approved the survey of new township lands, the Canada Townships, for granting to surviving participants and the heirs or descendants of the deceased (eldest male, or if none, eldest female) on application being made for a grant. (See also Watkins, *Soldiers in the Expedition*, p. 31f).

51. Order of General Court, May 25, 1691, in Moody & Simmons, *Selected Documents*, pp. 310-311.

52. Order of General Court, June 2, 1691, in Moody & Simmons, *Selected Documents*, p. 320.

53. Petition of the owners of the ketch *Mary Ann* and the brigantine *Mary*, June 25, 1691, and Record of General Court decision, October 3, 1691, in Moody & Simmons, *Selected Documents*, p. 333.

54. Massachusetts Archives (MA), Council Record, vol. 70, p. 165, Petition of Richard Arnall and Capt. Andrew Knott to His Excellency Sir William Phips, 1692. The earlier petitions can be found in MA, Council Record, Vol. 37, p. 183, July 7, 1691, and vol. 37, p. 69, October 22, 1691. No record of any additional payment has been found.

55. MA, Council Record, vol. 61, pp. 341, n.d., "To the Hono/ble

Assembly sitting in Boston for ye Probate of ye Massachusetts bay in New England, Petition of Nicholas Paige, John Pole, Daniel Allin, Mary Lamb late owners of the Ship Eliz. & Mary"; MA, Council Record, vol. 61, p. 342, n.d., "To the Hon/ble General Assembly sitting, Nicholas Paige, John Pole, Daniel Allin & Mary Lamb owners of the Ship Eliz. And Mary make by addition to their former Petition"; and MA, Council Record, vol. 2, pp. 239-240, Minutes of the Governor's Council, May 24, 1693, "Upon reading the Report of the Committee appointed to review and rectify the apprisement formerly made to the ship 'Elizabeth and Mary', with her appurtenances".

56. Mather, *The Life of Sir William Phips*, p. 82.

Phips' Amphibious Assault on Canada – 1690

Chapter Three

'Where Sovereignty Lay'

The Canada Expedition of 1690 was authorized, organized, and carried out during a period when the Massachusetts Bay Colony was under a provisional government, following on the overthrow of the Royal Government of Sir Edmund Andros in April 1689. It was a period of political upheaval marked by the flaring up of a long-standing dispute between the Crown and the General Court of the Massachusetts Bay Colony over 'where sovereignty lay'.

During the interregnum period, which lasted from April 1689 until the re-establishment of a royal government in May 1692, the Massachusetts Bay Colony was governed by a series of ad hoc bodies comprising a self-appointed "Council for Safety of the People and Conservation of the Peace"; a revived charter form of government basing its supposed sovereign power on a claim that the founding charter of the colony had been annulled illegally; a revived Charter government, which was authorized by a convention that espoused popular sovereignty, yet claimed only an interim authority pending receipt of the Crown's pleasure; and lastly, a provisional government authorized by the Crown and exercising a delegated sovereign power at the Crown's pleasure.

This chapter traces the long constitutional struggle of the 17th Century between the Crown and the General Court of the Massachusetts Bay Colony over 'where sovereignty lay'. It does so within the context of the worldview and religious frame of mind of the Puritans in an effort to better understand the constitutional struggle, as well as to determine where sovereign power resided at the time of the Phips' Canada Expedition of 1690.

Map Three.

Mainland English Colonies of North America, ca. 1690.
(Ken Watson, 2011)

Chapter Three

'Where Sovereignty Lay'

When the New England fleet arrived at Quebec on October 6, 1690, an ultimatum was issued to the French by Sir William Phips, the "General and Commander-in-chief in and over their Majesties' Forces of New-England, by Sea and Land". It demanded that the French surrender "in the Name and in the Behalf of Their Most Excellent Majesties, William and Mary, King and Queen of England, Scotland, France and Ireland", and "by Order of Their said Majesties' Government of the Massachuset-Colony in New-England".

The ultimatum seemingly claimed that Phips was acting under the sovereign authority of the Crown in demanding the surrender of Quebec, yet introduced an ambiguity in demanding that the French surrender by order of the government of the Massachusetts Bay Colony. The wording of the surrender ultimatum, however, was a product of the political evolution of the Massachusetts Bay Colony from its founding under a royal charter granted by Charles I in 1629, and revolutionary events in the colony following the Glorious Revolution of 1688 in England, all of which revolved around the issue of "where sovereignty lay".[1]

Sovereignty Concepts

As of the 17th Century political theorists had elaborated the modern concept of sovereignty as an absolute and indivisible political power possessed by a single ruler or ruling body with the authority to govern a people independent of, and unrestrained by, any superior authority. The principal sovereign powers were recognized as the right to make and to enforce the laws of a polity, to levy taxes, to coin money, to appoint the judiciary and law officers, to serve as a court of last resort, to command the military, and to make war and peace. However, the new absolutist concept of sovereignty continued to co-exist with an older medieval concept of sovereignty which was divisible, and could be delegated by the king in empowering another individual to govern a particular territory.

Under the feudal system of land tenure the king could grant royal powers – palatine powers – to a vassal-in-chief over a designated area of the king's realm in return for the vassal-in-chief fulfilling a duty of allegiance (primarily a specified military service) and fealty (by fulfilling his specific duties and obligations). A grant of palatine powers authorized and empowered the vassal-in-chief to govern his designated territory in perpetuity with royal powers, as an autonomous sovereign ruler, free from any temporal restraint and owing only an allegiance and fealty to the dominion sovereign.

Palatine powers were usually bestowed on a vassal-in-chief over territory on the periphery of the kingdom where there was a persistent external threat to the king's realm that needed to be continually addressed on the spot. As long as the vassal-in-chief maintained his allegiance by fulfilling the specific duties and obligations that he was sworn to uphold, then the delegated sovereignty remained unimpaired and irrevocable. A breaking of the oath of fidelity, however, constituted treason and justified the king resorting to force of arms to depose the vassal-in-chief.[2]

The concept of a divisible sovereignty persisted into the 17th Century in the founding of several colonies by the grant of a palatine charter. In several instances the king bestowed a charter that granted palatine powers in perpetuity to the projected proprietor or proprietors of a new colony on the periphery of the king's domain in North America. Once granted a palatine status under a royal charter, the proprietor(s) duly named, and his/their heirs, were authorized and empowered to govern the particular colonial territory in perpetuity as an autonomous sovereign power, independent of any superior authority, and subject only to a duty of allegiance to the Crown unless other duties and responsibilities were specified in the terms of the charter.[3]

Another means of establishing a colony as a legal entity was through the king granting a corporate charter. This approach was based on medieval corporation law, and had its origin in the practice of the king granting a written charter, and a seal, to establish and empower a corporation for a particular purpose. Merchant guilds, artisan guilds, and universities were incorporated through a royal charter, which recognized the newly-formed corporation as a legal entity within the kingdom, established its name and purpose, and bestowed specified privileges, liberties, and rights, and the authority to make and enforce rules and regulations for its members.

Similarly, the king could bestow a written charter, and a seal, on a town or a county to establish it as a legal corporate entity for the administration of justice and local government within its particular domain, or specified boundaries. A royal charter would provide the town or borough corporation, so formed, with the authority to pass by-laws, and would set forth the form of government and the rules governing the election of municipal officers, and the appointment of magistrates and a sheriff to enforce the by-laws passed by the governing body of the corporation.

Where corporations were concerned their authority rested ultimately on the royal authorization conveyed in their written charter. More generally, a legal corporation was characterized by: a corporate charter granted by the king in perpetuity, with the right of a perpetual succession in electing new members to fill vacancies; by the right to sue and be sued by name as a corporate entity; by a right to purchase and hold land in the name of the corporation; and by the right to establish and enforce by-laws for administering and governing its particular domain. In addition, a corporation possessed a corporate seal for authenticating letters and documents for legal purposes.[4]

A company could also be incorporated and empowered by a royal charter to govern a territory or colony for commercial trade and settlement purposes, with a duty to promote the dissemination of the Christian religion, but the powers granted were far from unlimited. The incorporated company was not a sovereign power.

The corporate charter would set forth the name, purpose, and jurisdiction of the incorporated company, as well as the offices to be occupied by election by the members, and might well empower that new legal entity with broad governing and magisterial powers within the colony, including the power to enact and enforce by-laws and regulations for governing the colony and for administrative purposes.

In sum, a corporate charter in incorporating a trading company would constitute it as a form of municipal government, with prescribed constitutional, political and magisterial powers to be exercised for the purposes of local government over the particular territory in which the company was operating.

Once incorporated a company was limited in its power and competence by the particular terms of the corporate charter; and the external relations of the colony – overseas trade and customs, war, and diplomacy – were governed by the Crown. A corporate charter might well be granted in perpetuity, but it was a contract enforceable in the law courts of England. A corporate charter could be revoked by the courts on the Crown proving in court that the corporation had exceeded the limits of the powers of its grant, or that the king had been deceived in the securing of the charter.[5]

Thus, in the 17th Century sovereignty could be conceptualized as either an absolute and indivisible power and right to rule vested solely in the king, or as a divisible power with the king able to grant palatine powers – sovereignty – to the proprietor(s) of a province or territory of the realm and his/their heirs in perpetuity, subject only to a prescribed duty of allegiance and fealty to the Crown.

On the other hand, the king could bestow a corporate charter on supplicants, and thereby incorporate a company for a particular purpose and empower it to serve as a local government over a particular colony or territory in the pursuit of that purpose. However, a corporation, once established by a royal charter, exercised only delegated powers of local government over the colony or territory, and was not a sovereign power *per se*.

At various stages in the political evolution of the Massachusetts Bay Colony disputes arose between the General Court and the Crown over 'where sovereignty lay'. The disputes arose principally from differing views as to the extent of the powers granted to the colonial government by the King Charles I in the Massachusetts Bay Charter of 1629, and reached a critical point following an insurrection in Boston on April 18, 1689. At that time, just a year before the Phips' Canada Expedition was authorized, colonists began to put forth a new concept of 'where sovereignty lay'.

The Charter of 1629

In 1629 King Charles I granted a charter to a joint-stock trading company, the Massachusetts Bay Company, for the establishment of a plantation on Massachusetts Bay in New England, and endowed the corporation so formed with extensive powers to govern the plantation. The corporation, then headquartered in England, was bestowed with the authority:

> *"to make, ordeine, and establishe all manner of wholesome and reasonable orders, lawes, statutes, and ordinances, directions, and instructions, not contrarie to the lawes of this our realm of England, as well for setling of the forms and ceremonies of government and magistracy fitt and necessary for the said plantation, and the inhabitants there, and for nameing and stiling of all sortes of officers, both superior and inferior, which they shall finde needeful for that governement and plantation, and the distinguishing and setting*

forth of the severall duties, powers, and lymytts of every such office and place." [6]

The charter further specified that the laws governing the company and the colony were to be established by a "Great and General Court" composed of the stockholders of the Massachusetts Bay Company, so-called "freemen", meeting in the General Court four times per year. In the interim between meetings of the General Court, the affairs of the company and the colony were to be managed by a governor, deputy governor, and eighteen "assistants" who were to be elected annually, for a one-year term, by the freemen meeting at the General Court.

The only limit on the corporation's authority was that none of the laws enacted for the governance of the Massachusetts Bay Colony were to be contrary to the laws of England. There were no stated limits on the exercise of judicial powers or executive actions.[7]

The proprietors of the Massachusetts Bay Company were Puritans, or Calvinist Anglicans, who believed that the Reformation would not be completed until the national church, the Church of England, was "purified' with the removal of its episcopal polity and other 'Popish' remnants of the liturgy and clerical vestments retained on breaking away from the Roman Catholic Church. However, by the late 1620s, the rise of Arminianism within the established Church, the purging of Puritan clergy from their livings, and the profligacy of England under Charles I, led the proprietors of the Massachusetts Bay Company to look to establishing a settlement in the New World where they might put their scriptural beliefs into practice.

By that time Puritanism rested solidly on a belief in God's absolute sovereignty over the world, predestination, and the concept of the covenant of grace, which together entailed a belief in God's sovereign control over man's life, his salvation, and history. The Puritans believed in the Calvinist doctrine of absolute predestination – the belief that some are predestined to everlasting life by God's eternal and unchangeable decree; and that others are foreordained to everlasting death.

In contrast, Arminians believed in man's free will, and held to a belief in a conditional predestination – that God had decreed that all individuals who had faith in Christ, and persevered in faith and obedience to the end, would attain salvation through the Holy Spirit. Only those who had faith, in freely choosing Christ as their redeemer, would be saved.

For the Puritans, there was no room for compromise with the Arminian clergy of the Church of England who rejected the Calvinist doctrine of predestination in favour of a belief in free will; who upheld the spiritual authority of the episcopacy and The Book of Common Prayer liturgy; and who adhered to the established Church rituals and clerical vestments.

In rejecting the spiritual authority of the episcopacy, the Puritans held to a belief in the concept of the covenant, or Covenant of Grace, which pervaded and shaped their view of both church and state. They believed that a people or a community of believers who freely chose to obey God's law as set forth in Scriptures, entered into a Covenant of Grace directly with God, "the Sovereign of the Universe", and became a 'chosen people' or 'community of saints'.

A covenanted people, so formed, would prosper or suffer the wrath of God in so far as they, and their government, upheld or breached the Covenant to obey His laws. Indeed, history was regarded as the visible working out of divine Providence in the world, by which God through direct intervention blessed the chosen people with gifts of His Grace, or punished them with various afflictions directly proportional to the degree of their transgression of His laws.

The predestinated elect, who had received God's grace, would covenant or gather together with other 'visible saints' in a congregation to receive the sacraments of baptism and communion, and to hear the Word of God as declared in Scripture.

Each congregation, so gathered, was independent of any outside authority, had spiritual autonomy, and elected and ordained its own minister by ratifying 'the call' received by a member of the elect to preach the Word. Thus the Puritans rejected episcopal ordination through the traditional 'laying on of hands' by a bishop of Christ's Church, and rejected episcopal authority within the established Church of England. In effect, ministerial authority was based on the consent of the gathered saints, the members of the congregation, rather than ordination by a bishop of the established Church.

Under the first Governor of the Massachusetts Bay Company, John Winthrop, several convoys of ships carrying Puritan settlers were dispatched from England in 1629 and 1630, accompanied in the first instance by the Charter, to establish a religious community on Massachusetts Bay -- a religious settlement governed by the saints gathered together in a Covenant of Grace.

The plantation was intended to serve as a model religious community, a 'City upon a Hill', which in being governed by God's law, in both church and state, would prosper and speed the reformation in England by inspiring others to imitate the 'holy experiment'.[8]

What is more, New England would be a nursery where soldiers and seamen could be raised and trained for the Holy War which the Puritans were convinced would have to be waged in defence of Protestantism against the Catholic Powers, and the forces of the Catholic Counter-Reformation, which were at war seemingly everywhere in Europe in seeking to conquer the Protestant countries and eradicate Protestantism.[9]

Steps were taken, immediately upon arrival in the New World, to form a church-state government – a theocracy – based on the

Charter of 1629 and the laws of Holy Scripture. The General Court was established as the supreme legislative and judicial authority in the colony, and acts were passed deeming all adult male members of the Puritan congregation to be "freemen", who were eligible to participate in the General Court and in the annual election of the Governor, Deputy Governor, and Assistants.

When the direct participation of the congregation in the government of the colony proved unwieldy, the General Court was divided into two houses: a Court of Assistants (the Governor, Deputy Governor, and the Assistants), who were to be elected directly by the freemen of the colony; and a House of Representatives in which sat deputies, who were to be elected by the freemen, with two deputies representing each town in the colony.

All laws had to be passed by both houses, but the executive and judicial functions were exercised solely by the Court of Assistants acting in the name of the General Court. The members of the Court of Assistants also served as magistrates in the county courts, and as Justices of the Peace in the quarter-sessions. In the General Court, the Assistants were often referred to simply as "magistrates". All judgements of the courts were based on the laws of Scripture rather than English common law; and writs and processes were issued in the name of the General Court rather than the King's name.

In the Massachusetts Bay Colony all public authority came to rest on the Charter of 1629 which was transformed into the constitution of government, and government acts and court proceedings were devoid of any reference to royal authority. The exception was the Oath of Allegiance to the King, which was administered to the elected magistrates (Assistants) and deputies on taking their seats in the General Court.[10] In sum, as one contemporary attorney noted in commenting on how the Massachusetts Bay Colony's system of government had evolved:

> *"In their general courts and quarter-sessions, they exercised all the powers of parliament, king's-bench, common-pleas, chancery, high-commission, star-chamber, and all other courts of England ...."*[11]

During the English Civil War (1642-1651), which pitted the King against Parliament and cost Charles I both his throne and his life, the Massachusetts Bay Colony had functioned as a sovereign power, totally independent of the Crown of England. The General Court dispensed with the Oath of Allegiance to the King as early as 1643 and substituted an oath of allegiance to the Charter government.

Moreover, following the abolition of the English monarchy, in 1649, and thereafter under the Protectorate of Oliver Cromwell, the Massachusetts Bay Colony had gone its own way in functioning as a self-governing republic, all but ignored by the English government which was preoccupied with affairs in Europe.

When the English monarchy was restored under Charles II in 1660, the new King had no role at all in the government of the Massachusetts Bay Colony, and any claim of the English Crown to the allegiance of the colony or any legal limits on the authority of the colonial corporation had lain dormant for several decades.[12]

After the restoration of the Stuart monarchy, in 1660, a twenty-five-year struggle ensued in which the General Court resisted the efforts of the Crown to assert royal authority in the colony. Given that the Puritans of the Massachusetts Bay Colony were a covenanted people, the General Court could not but have been alarmed by, and offered resistance to, any effort to assert the sovereignty of the Crown.

Any assertion of royal sovereignty in the colony whether over military defence, or in ensuring that the laws, which had been established by the General Court, were not in contravention of the laws of England, was seen as a threat to the theocratic government that the Puritans had established in the Massachusetts Bay Colony. It would deprive their government of patronage power over militia appointments and command of the military; and would substitute the laws of man for the laws of "the Sovereign of the Universe" and 'His fundamental law as set forth in Holy Scripture'. Moreover, any assertion of royal power was a threat to the hegemony of the established church polity of the Massachusetts Puritans.

The threat to the Puritan religious establishment was all the more real as the English government after the Restoration was dominated by Royalists who abhorred Puritanism. In England, the 'Cavalier Parliament' passed a series of acts that re-instituted the traditional doctrines, theology, episcopacy, and liturgy in the established Church of England, and required all public worship to be in accordance with The Book of Common Prayer. Dissenters were excluded from teaching positions, and the new laws required that all elected members of governments and of corporations be adherents of the Anglican Communion. As a result, in England over 2,000 Puritan ministers, and numerous Puritan magistrates, were forced from their positions.

Another more general concern of the Puritans was that Charles II, although a Protestant, was known to have Roman Catholic sympathies, and his brother and heir-apparent James, Duke of York, was rumoured to be a staunch Roman Catholic which later, in 1669, he would publically confirm.[13]

Somewhat earlier the Puritans of the Massachusetts Bay Company had united with the Separatists, or Independent Puritans of the Plymouth, Connecticut and New Haven colonies of New England to agree on a statement of their common faith and doctrine of church government: the Cambridge Platform (1648). It was based on an earlier statement – the Westminster Confession – promulgated by English Puritan divines in 1646.

The Cambridge Platform confirmed the Massachusetts Puritans

belief in Calvinist theology; their adherence to the congregational system of church government; and their upholding of the doctrine that the civil authority had a duty to enforce religious orthodoxy within the state (the colony) by supporting the Church of God and punishing perverse religious opinions.[14]

As such, the Puritans of the Massachusetts Bay Colony were clearly fearful that any imposition of royal authority in the colony would bring the establishment of the episcopal Church of England in place of the Puritan churches, which enjoyed establishment prerogatives in the colony under a theocratic government that prosecuted religious dissenters.[15]

To forestall the possibility of the Crown appointing a royal governor in authority over the Massachusetts Bay Colony, the General Court issued, in June 1661, a declaration of liberties and duties of allegiance to the newly restored Crown. While recognizing that allegiance was owed to the English Crown, the declaration at the same time proclaimed the independence of the Massachusetts Bay Colony government within the colonial empire on the premise that Charles I, in granting the Charter of 1629, had bestowed on the Massachusetts Bay Company a grant of an absolute power of self-government; and that sovereignty once delegated was irrevocable.[16]

The authority of the General Court, elected by the freemen of the colony, was declared to extend into all areas of government – civil, judicial, and ecclesiastical – with the right to place and empower all office holders and public officials. No exterior power (and by implication the Crown) had the right to intervene or impose other laws, nor was there any right of appeal beyond the General Court with the sole exception of a single restriction enunciated in the Charter of 1629: viz.

> *"The Governor, Deputy Governor, Assistants, and select representatives or deputies have full power and authoritie, both legislative and executive, for the government of all the people heere, wither inhabitants*

> *or straingers, both concerning eclesiasticks and in civils, without appeale, excepting lawe or lawes repugnant to the lawes of England."*

Although the Charter of 1629 did not bestow any military authority on the General Court, the Court claimed the right to take whatever military measures were required to defend the colony against attack by external powers: viz.

> *"The government is priviledged by all fitting meanes (yea, and if neede be, by force of armes) to defend themselves, both by land and sea, against all such person or persons as shall at any time attempt or enterprise the destruction, invasion, dettriment, or annoyance of this plantation, or the inhabitants therein, besides other priviledges mentioned in the pattent, not heere expressed."*

It is clear, however, that such military measures were to be undertaken in the name of the King in defence of His Majesties' realm. In essence, the General Court could not but recognize the King as the "soveraigne lord" of the colony. It was the Crown that had bestowed the Charter creating the Massachusetts Bay Company; and that granted the General Court its powers of governance in all matters civil and judicial, but not ecclesiastical.

The General Court's professed allegiance to the Crown was circumscribed and limited, as enunciated in the declaration, to maintaining and defending the King's colony against conquest by any foreign power, to resisting insurrections aimed at overthrowing the monarch, and to promoting peace and prosperity among the people entrusted to their governance, as well as to propagating the Protestant religion.

The extent of the allegiance owed to the Crown was set forth in three main clauses:

> *"1. Wee ought to uphold and to our power maineteine this place, as of right belonging to our soveraigne lord the king, as holden of his majesties mannor of East Greenwich, and not to subject the same to any forreigne prince or potentate whatsoever.*
>
> *2. Wee ought to endeavor the preservation of his majesties royall person, realmes, and dominions, and so farre as lieth in us, to discover and prevent all plotts and conspiracies against the same.*
>
> *3. Wee ought to seeke the peace and prosperitie of our king and nation, by a faith full discharge in the governing of this people commited to our care: -- ..."*[17]

The General Court was prepared to govern in the King's name, and to provide military support in defence of the King's dominions, but recognized no right of the Crown to interfere with the established system of government in the Massachusetts Bay Colony, its laws, ordinances, or judicial rulings. Moreover, the General Court did not recognize any limits on its exercise of military power, nor admit any right of the Crown to command the militia of the colony, or to intervene in its ecclesiastical affairs.

In the Massachusetts Bay Colony the General Court mustered the militia for service and appointed the colonels and lieutenant colonels of militia regiments; and the officers of the militia companies were chosen by the soldiers of each company subject to the approval of the General Court. Militia companies also were posted to the frontier garrisons by order of the General Court.[18]

More generally, during the early 17th Century the New England colonies provided their own defence against the Indians on their frontiers. The Crown supplied ordnance and gunpowder for the defence of the colony, but not soldiers; and the Royal Navy assisted armed merchantmen and colonial warships in protecting coastal shipping from pirates, as well as protected colonial shipping on the high seas against enemy warships and privateers in time of war.[19]

The position adopted by the General Court in their declaration of allegiance to the Crown amounted to a claim that Charles I in the granting the Massachusetts Bay Charter of 1629 had bestowed palatine powers on the proprietors of the Charter, the Massachusetts Bay Company. In effect, the General Court was claiming that the Crown had delegated sovereignty to the company within the territory of the Massachusetts Bay Colony; and that the colony was a feudal fiefdom, or palatinate, within which the proprietors of the Charter held sovereignty in perpetuity.

Thus, the colony owed allegiance to the Crown, in being bound to defend the king's person and realm, but enjoyed the possession and exercise of an independent sovereign power within the territory of the colony.[20] Indeed, several of the North American colonies were founded on charters granting palatine powers including, for example, Maryland (1632), and subsequently Carolina (1663, 1665), but that was hardly the case with the Massachusetts Bay Colony charter.[21]

Where the Province of Maryland was concerned the Charter granted by Charles I in 1632 conveyed palatine powers, or sovereignty, in perpetuity to the proprietor, Caecilius Calvert, Baron of Baltimore, his heirs and assigns. Baltimore was granted "as ample Rights, Jurisdictions, Privileges, Prerogatives, Royalties, Liberties, Immunities, and royal Rights, and temporal Franchises whatsoever, as well by Sea as by Land, within the Region, Islands, Islets, and Limits, [of the said Province], to be had, exercised, used, and enjoyed, as any Bishop of Durham with the Bishoprick or County Palatine of Durham, in our Kingdom of England".

The Maryland Charter granted Baron Baltimore a "free and absolute power" to make laws "with the Advice, Assent, and Approbation of the Free-men of the same Province, or the greater part of them, or of their Delegates or Deputies", to establish courts (both civil and criminal), to appoint judges and law officers, to enforce the laws, and to impose martial law in time of war or insurrection.

In addition, he was granted "free and plenary powers" to incorporate towns and boroughs, to confer titles and honours, to build harbours and sea-ports, to establish places of worship of the Church of England, to raise troops, to appoint officers of the militia, to wage war, to fish the waters, to open mines and quarries. He was empowered, as well, to export the province's products to markets in England and re-export from there to friendly foreign countries after a year, to levy taxes and customs duties on the trade of the province, to tax the inhabitants, and to hold and sell the land in fee simple.

By the Charter of 1632 the Maryland Province, with all its resources, was held in fealty to the Crown; and both the proprietor and inhabitants of the province owed allegiance to the King. Moreover, the proprietor was required to pay an annual rent to the Crown consisting of two Indian arrows and a fifth-part royalty on all gold and silver ore discovered in the province.

The Maryland Charter placed only one restraint on the "free, full and absolute" power of the province to make laws: viz. "That the Laws aforesaid be consonant to Reason, and be not repugnant or contrary, but (so far as conveniently may be) agreeable to the Laws, Statutes, Customs, and Rights of this Our Kingdom of England". Moreover, outside of the territory of the province, when trading with England and friendly foreign countries, provincials had to pay the same customs duties and taxes to the Crown as the King's subjects in England who were engaged in overseas trade.

In effect, the government of the Province of Maryland was sovereign within its own territory, and exercised a delegated sovereignty free of any limitations or interference from the Crown; yet owed allegiance to the King, who retained an overall "Sovereign Dominion" in keeping with the medieval concept of divisible sovereignty.[22] This was likewise the case with the Province of Carolina, which was established by a royal charter granted by Charles II in 1663, and again in 1665 upon the enlargement of the new province.

The Carolina charters granted palatine powers to the proprietors of the new Province of Carolina equivalent to those enjoyed by the Bishop of Durham in England. Indeed, the successive Carolina charters were almost identical to the earlier Maryland Charter in the setting forth the specific sovereign powers and rights bestowed on the proprietors of the new provincial territory by the Crown; the duty of allegiance owed to the Crown of England; and the annual rent to be paid to the Crown which for Carolina consisted of a payment of 20 marks and a one quarter royalty on all gold and silver ore discovered in the province.

Given its position on the exposed frontier with Spanish Florida the military powers of the new Province of Carolina were set forth in greater detail than in the Maryland Charter. Thus the Carolina proprietors were specifically granted the right to erect forts, fortresses, castles and other fortifications, and to furnish them with "ordnance, powder, shot, armour, and all other weapons, ammunition, and habiliments of war, both defensive and offensive", and "to levy, muster, and train up all sorts of men" for military service. The Carolina proprietors were empowered as well, in making war, to "pursue the enemies aforesaid [enemies, pirates, and robbers], as well by sea, as by land; yea, even without the limits of the said province".[23]

In sum, the proprietors of the Maryland Province and the Province of Carolina, respectively, held palatine powers – sovereignty – over their respective territories under their founding charters, which had been granted by the King in keeping with the medieval concept of a divisible sovereignty. This was decidedly not the case with Massachusetts Bay Company.

The Massachusetts Bay Charter of 1629 was a corporate charter incorporating a trading company. The charter granted the proprietors of the Massachusetts Bay Company, and their successors, the right to govern and administer the territory of the Massachusetts Bay plantation in perpetuity, but it was not a grant of palatine powers conveying sovereignty over the territory of the colony.

The Massachusetts Bay Company was empowered by its founding charter with wide political and magisterial powers to govern and administer the colony as a local 'municipal' government. And although the General Court did govern the colony for decades after its inception as a *de facto* self-governing sovereign power, acting independent of the English Crown, it was not a *de jure* sovereign power.

The Massachusetts Bay Charter of 1629 was a corporate charter, a form of contract entered into in England and enforceable by the law courts in England. Thus, it could be annulled by the courts on the Crown bringing suit against the proprietors and proving that the terms of the corporate charter had been violated.[24] Moreover, at the Restoration of the Stuarts in 1660, the Crown had ample reason to believe that a number of the colonial governments, foremost amongst them the Massachusetts Bay Colony, were exercising powers of government far beyond what had been granted in their founding charters.

Commencing in 1664, King Charles II sought to assert royal authority in the North American colonies through requesting that the colonial governments surrender their respective charters for revision. The purpose was to enable the Crown to ascertain the actual powers, rights, and liberties which had been granted to each colony in its particular charter, and to modify the charters in order to recognize the sovereignty of the Crown in a precise and meaningful way.

Initially the King aimed simply to ensure that royal authority was exerted through having the governor of each colony nominated, or approved, by the Crown; through placing the colonial militia under the command of an officer nominated or recommended by the Crown; and through confining the authority exercised by each colonial government to the actual powers granted in its founding charter.[25]

This effort failed to resolve the sovereignty issue. The Massachusetts Bay Colony refused to surrender its charter, and declined to negotiate with the Crown's representatives. When the Crown sought to impose colonial trade laws – the Navigation Acts, or Acts of Trade – on the North American colonies, the General Court again asserted its claim to an absolute sovereign power in civil matters in denying the jurisdiction of England laws in their colony.

An open conflict was avoided when the colony eventually passed the Navigation Acts as acts of the General Court to be enforced by its own authority, rather than by the royal authority. At the same time, the General Court strengthened the oath of allegiance to the Charter Government which had replaced the Oath of Allegiance to the King during the English Civil War period.

Throughout the decade of the 1670s the issue of 'where sovereignty lay' remained unresolved. The king and royal officials maintained that the Crown possessed sovereignty over the territory of the Massachusetts Bay Colony; whereas the General Court maintained that sovereignty over the territory of the Massachusetts Bay plantation had been irrevocably delegated to the proprietors of the Massachusetts Bay Company by the Crown.

As the trade of New England underwent a rapid expansion

the issue became more acute. The Massachusetts Bay Colony continued to assert its independence of English laws, and failed to fully enforce the Navigation Acts governing foreign trade and shipping. Moreover, the General Court retained the revenues, which were raised under the acts from duties on imports and from fines and forfeitures.

The resistance of the General Court to efforts by the Crown and, after 1675, by the newly established Board of Trade and Plantations, to regulate and tax colonial trade, and a comparatively lax enforcement of the Navigation Acts by the other colonies, spurred further efforts to bring charter governments in the American and Caribbean colonies under royal authority.

It was evident to the Board of Trade that the sovereignty of the Crown would have to be effectively established in the government of each colony in order to secure an enforcement of the trade laws; and that this was particularly the case with the Massachusetts Bay Colony.[26]

Failing to achieve a resolution through negotiations, in June 1663 the Crown commenced a legal action before the Court of King's Bench proceeding by writ of *quo warranto* against the Massachusetts Bay Company for having exceeded the liberties granted in its Charter.

At the same time, in a last minute effort to avoid legal action, a royal declaration was issued which promised that if the colony would voluntarily surrender its charter for revision, all existing property rights would be respected and changes to the Charter would be minimal, confined to simply clarifying the colony's dependence on the Crown. This the colony refused to do, and engaged a London barrister to defend its patent in Court.

During the negotiations process the writ of *quo warranto* expired, and the Crown then entered a writ of *scire facias et alias* in

Chancery Court, seeking an annulment of the Charter on the grounds that the King had been deceived in his grant. In June 1684 the charter was declared annulled by the Court, but the decree was suspended until the fall of 1684 to give the Governor and Massachusetts Bay Company time to appear in Court.

Owing to a delay in their London barrister forwarding word of the new legal action to Boston, insufficient time remained for the Massachusetts Bay Company to go to London to plead their case. Thus on October 23, 1684, the Governor and Massachusetts Bay Company having failed to appear in Court, the Charter was declared "cancelled, vacated, and annihilated", ending the legal existence of the charter government of the Massachusetts Bay Colony.[27]

The annulment of the Massachusetts Bay Charter of 1629 marked the culmination of Charles II's effort to establish royal authority in the Massachusetts colony. With his death, in 1685, it was left to his successor, King James II, to settle the sovereignty issue through imposing a royal government on the Massachusetts Bay Colony. In the interim, the General Court continued to govern as the *de facto* sovereign government of the Massachusetts Bay Colony in the absence of any direction from the Crown.

The last annual election for the deputies of the House of Representatives was held on May 12, 1686, followed by the election of the magistrates of the Court of Assistants (Governor, Deputy Governor, and Assistants). Two days later, a ship arrived in Boston Harbour with a royal commission appointing a sixteen-man Council, headed by Joseph Dudley of Boston, to govern the Massachusetts Bay Colony, New Hampshire, Maine, and the Narragansett Country (or King's Province) pending the appointment of a royal governor.

The General Court met to examine the legal judgement that annulled the Charter of 1629, and the royal commission of Joseph Dudley, and then adjourned on May 21, 1686, acquiescing in the royal settlement.[28] The Puritan establishment would seek to have the annulment of the Charter overturned by legal action in London rather than risk an open conflict, if not a war, with the Crown.

The formation of a new royal province was but part of a broader on-going effort by James II to consolidate royal power and extend royal authority, through annulling by court action the charters of the various overseas colonies, as well as the ancient town corporations in England. In June 1686, a second royal commission extended the borders of the new royal province by incorporating Rhode Island, Connecticut, New York, and New Jersey, with the Massachusetts Bay Colony, New Plymouth, New Hampshire, Maine, and the Narraganset Country, into a new "Dominion of New England in America".

Sir Edmund Andros was appointed as Captain General and Governor-in-Chief to govern the new province with the advice of the sixteen-man Council, and granted full power and authority to make laws, statutes and ordinances "for the public peace, welfare and good government", to establish Admiralty Courts and Courts of Judicature both civil and criminal, and to appoint Justices of the Peace, Sheriffs, and other administrative officers, as well as the power to raise troops for the defence of the province.

In dispensing with representative assemblies, and having secured annulments of the various colonial charters through legal action in the courts, the formation of the new royal government of the Dominion of New England in America clearly established the Crown's sovereign power in the American colonies unabridged and unlimited.[29] The sovereignty of the Crown, however, was no sooner clearly established than the new royal government was overthrown.

The Insurrection of April 18, 1689

In early April 1689, the citizens of Boston received stunning news. Some five months earlier, on November 5, 1688, Prince William of Orange, the Stadholder (chief of state) of the Calvinist Dutch Republic (Republic of the United Netherlands) had landed in England with a Protestant army of 15,000 men and marched on London, causing the Roman Catholic monarch, King James II, to flee the country.

Moreover, Bostonians learned that on October 10, 1688, prior to invading England, Prince William had issued a Declaration that declared his intention to restore English liberties, to maintain the Protestant Religion, and to restore the ancient charters that the courts had annulled under the Stuarts (Charles II, and James II). What is more, the Declaration called on all magistrates unjustly removed from office by the Stuarts, to resume their duties.

Such a declaration was an invitation to revolt in New England where the government of Sir Edmund Andros was extremely unpopular. Leading members of the former General Court were far from reconciled to the new royal government based on what they perceived as the illegal annulment of their Charter, and hence the imposition of what they regarded as an arbitrary government by James II. And in Boston, the merchants were incensed by the Andros government's rigid enforcement of the Navigation Acts in collecting customs duties and curbing smuggling.

More generally, public discontent had been aroused by the government's questioning of the legality of the land grants which had been made by the former General Court; its claim that vacant lands were Crown lands to be granted at the Crown's pleasure; and its imposition of high taxes, without the consent of any elected representatives of the people, in order to maintain and strengthen the frontier garrisons defending the colonies against Indian attacks.

There was resentment as well at the government's apparent lack of success in suppressing Indian raids, at Andros' befriending of the Indians in an unsuccessful effort to pacify them, and at the rumoured maltreatment of militia men who were serving on the frontier under officers of the regular British army.

The Puritan clergy and their congregations were further incensed that the government of Sir Edmund Andros seemingly favoured the Anglican minority, through commandeering a congregational church in Boston for Anglican services, in appointing Anglicans to key administrative positions, and in purging Puritans from the higher ranks of the militia and replacing them with Anglicans. As of the spring of 1689 the Andros government had succeeded in alienating all but a small minority of the population of New England.[30]

On hearing what had transpired in England, and the contents of Prince William's Declaration, Bostonians took to the streets. On April 18, 1689, an uprising was launched against the royal government that James II had appointed to govern the new Dominion of New England. Supported by the local militia, the insurgents seized and imprisoned Sir Edmund Andros and his appointed Council.[31]

In an attempt to justify their actions, the leading insurgents immediately issued a declaration. It questioned the legality of the annulment of the Charter of 1629, and the supplanting of the former General Court government by that of Sir Edmund Andros, on the grounds that the colony had not been represented by legal counsel at the judicial court hearings in London. The declaration also stated that the citizens of Boston had acted to defend 'English Liberties' against an arbitrary government, which had been imposed upon them by a 'Popish King', King James II.

Among the specific charges made was that the Andros government had imposed taxes without the consent of the people, as expressed through a representative assembly; had failed to adequately defend the colony's frontiers against attack by the Indian allies of the French; and had given government appointments to placemen, who gained preferment and lands at the expense of the colonists whose land titles were called into question.

The insurgents were careful to avoid any potential charge of treason for rebelling against the Crown. To that end, the declaration expressed the people's loyalty to King William, and stated that Governor Andros and his Council would be retained in confinement pending receipt of direction from the King and Parliament on how the prisoners should be brought to justice.[32]

In response to the overthrow of the royal government, fifteen prominent Boston merchants and leading members of the former General Court, established a "Council for Safety of the People and Conservation of the Peace" to provide an orderly government for the Massachusetts Bay Colony. The Council immediately appointed port collectors and local officials, assigned militia officers to their commands, and declared that "for the present exigence", Council members were empowered to serve as Justices of the Peace.[33]

The intention of the Council was to act as an *ad hoc* interim government while petitioning the Crown for a restoration of the Charter of 1629. In London, the colony's agent, the Reverend Increase Mather, who had been sent to England to contest the legality of the Charter's annulment, began to lobby the new Court of William III and Parliament for a restoration of the Charter. The ultimate purpose was to secure the re-establishment of an independent charter government in the Massachusetts Bay Colony.[34]

In the interim, the Council for Safety under the presidency of Simon Bradstreet – the last governor elected under the old charter system of government in May 1686 – sought to gain public support for their assumption of power following a resort to the force of arms. The Council called on each town to send one or two representatives to a meeting in Boston on May 9th, such representatives to be "fully empowered then and there to consult, advise, join, and give their assistance" to the Council in acting as an interim government.[35]

The Revolutionary Government of Massachusetts

On meeting in Boston, on May 10th, the town representatives issued a declaration stating that the Governor, Deputy Governor, Assistants, and Deputies, elected "according to our Charter Rights" to the last General Court in May 1686, were the legitimate government of the colony until new elections could be held. In effect, the town representatives refused to recognize the authority of the self-appointed Council for Safety, and wanted to revive the last General Court government.[36]

This stance by the town representatives threatened to dramatically inflame the political situation as it would re-established a government based on a charter that had been legally annulled by the courts; and that had been dissolved by the Crown. It also entailed the abandonment of the Council for Safety's cautious approach in proclaiming loyalty to the Crown, while establishing an *ad hoc* interim government to maintain order until instructions were received from the Crown.

After much debate, it was agreed to consult the people at large concerning the declaration of the town representatives, and to convene a second meeting of the town representatives in Boston on May 22nd to decide the form of government. It was agreed that the Council for Safety would remain in being until that date, and could take whatever measures were necessary to defend the colony should an emergency occur. However, the town representatives insisted that if orders arrived from England concerning the settling of a form of government, they were to be recalled and consulted before any new administration was established.[37]

Thereafter, the Council for Safety forwarded a loyalty Address to Prince William petitioning for a restoration of the former charter government. The Address sought to justify the insurrection of April 18th, and the imprisonment of the Sir Edmund Andros and his Council. It stated that His Majesties' call on the English Nation to defend their ancient English liberties and the Protestant religion against an arbitrary government, had excited the colonists to rise against an equally arbitrary government imposed when they were deprived of their charter government. Having imitated Prince William's noble effort, they now wanted only to "Share in the Universal Restoration of Charters, and English Liberties" so as to enjoy their former rights and privileges under the Charter of 1629.[38]

Following the Glorious Revolution of 1688 in England, the attitude of the New England Puritans underwent a dramatic transformation where the Crown was concerned. For the Puritans, the landing of Prince William of Orange in England, and the subsequent overthrow of the royal government of the 'Popish King', James II, was nothing less than an act of Providence, an act of divine intervention. Englishmen, both in England and New England, were viewed as sharing in a common deliverance from an arbitrary government bent on extirpating the Protestant religion and the rights and privileges of Englishmen.

Prince William was seen as the saviour of Protestantism, and the defender of the 'true faith' against the efforts of the Roman Catholic powers, led by Louis XIV of France, to eradicate the Protestant religion from Europe. Following the Glorious Revolution, loyalty to the Crown could be expressed in all sincerity by the General Court, which fully expected that the Charter of 1629 would be restored once the new monarch was ensconced on the throne.[39]

None the less, the Massachusetts Bay Puritans remained adamant in their belief that they could not accept the imposition of any royal government that would threaten their theocracy, the rule of God's law, or the independence and self-government that they had enjoyed under the Charter.

In late May 1689, word was received in Boston that a

"Convention Parliament", which met in London on January 22nd, had officially bestowed the Crown on King William III (Prince William of Orange) and Queen Mary (Princess Mary) as joint sovereigns. The transfer of sovereignty was justified on the grounds that James II in fleeing England had abandoned his throne, and, by doing so, had abdicated and left Parliament to determine the succession. It was also alleged that James II had violated his Coronation Oath in failing to respect the established laws of England.

The new joint monarchs established a Protestant succession in England. Princess Mary, the eldest daughter of James II, had been raised a Protestant, and her husband Prince William of Orange, a Dutch Calvinist, had led two grand alliances of European powers resisting by force of arms the expansionist policies of Louis XIV of Catholic France.[40]

With a Protestant succession in England, the Council for Safety was content to await instructions from the Crown as to the form of government to be established in the colony, and was confident that the Charter would be restored.[41] The country towns and villages, however, soon took control of events, spurred by a different view of 'where sovereignty lay'.

During the month of May 1689, at town meetings throughout the colony, the issue of the form of government was debated at length, and resulted in the vast majority of the towns petitioning the Council for an immediate re-establishment of the charter government. On May 24th, the town representatives and the Council for Safety met in Boston to determine what was to be done. The significance of the issue under debate was evident in the meeting being designated a "convention", in imitation of the Convention Parliament that had bestowed the Crown on King William and Queen Mary.[42]

At the Convention the elected Town representatives voted a resolution that expressed the hope that King William would restore their Charter patent and privileges, but declared "that the

Dependence and Method of Settlement of the said Government in the present Juncture lieth wholly in the People". Hence the resolution called for an immediate reinstatement of charter government in keeping with the expressed will of the towns, and a resumption of power by the Governor, Deputy-Governor, and Assistants elected in the last election of May 1686. It was further stated that should the Crown subsequently seek any alteration in the charter government, then the towns must be informed "so they may be Consulted with in order to obtain their Approbation and Compliance".[43]

Here was a truly revolutionary declaration of popular sovereignty. Government was to be constituted by the people, and altered only with the approval of the people. Moreover, the government that the town representatives were demanding, a re-established charter government, was no doubt envisaged as one that would function virtually independent of the English Crown. In effect, they sought to re-establish a charter government in the full expectation that it would act as a *de facto* sovereign power, as it had in the past, with only a perfunctory acknowledgement of allegiance to the English Crown.[44]

In response the former magistrates, who had been elected in May1686, declared that they "from the Present Necessity and for Satisfaction of the People do Consent and Accept the Care and Government of the people of this Colony, according to the Rules of the Charter". They would govern with the assistance of the representatives of the Towns until instructions were received from England as to the form of government to be established. However, once the resolution was passed by a vote of the Convention of Representatives, and ordered to be printed for public dissemination, the restored magistrates affixed a notation declaring that the signatories "do not intend an Assumption of Charter Government; nor Would be so Understood."[45]

By this manoeuvre, and the wording of the declaration, the Council members sought to avoid a potential conflict with the Crown, and the risk of any future attainder for treason; and yet, at the same time, they sought to appease two important political forces: the merchant community, which wanted to avoid any conflict that might disrupt trade with the mother country; and the country representatives, who demanded a restoration of charter government on the basis of a belief in popular sovereignty.[46]

The new government consisted of a Council (the former Council for Safety reduced in number and reorganized to include only the former magistrates elected in 1686) and a Convention of Representatives embodying the elected Town representatives, with both bodies to be renewed subsequently through annual elections. No sooner was the May 24, 1689, declaration published than the representatives objected to the magistrates' disclaimer of any intent to restore the charter government.

At a meeting of the new Council and Convention of Representatives on June 5th the representatives refused to pass any legislation until the magistrates responded to the will of the people by declaring a full restoration of charter government. The representatives submitted a declaration to the Governor and Council stating that the authority of the interim government rested solely on the sovereign will of the people expressed through their representatives.

The declaration referred to the magistrates having consented to "Accept the care and Government of the people" on May 24th, and concluded:

> *"We do now humbly pray Considering the present Circumstances of this Colony you would be pleased by Vertue of the Authority devolved on You, by us the Representatives of the Several Towns in this Colony to Accept Government according to our Charter Rules by the Names of Governr. and Council for the Massachusets Colony, and exercise such Authority in the said Colony, as was formally Used by the Laws made by our Charter Government (excepting such as*

> *may be Judged repugnant to the Laws of England) until farther Orders from England; ....*"[47]

Having but little choice, if government business were to continue to be conducted, the magistrates fully re-established the charter government of the old Massachusetts Bay Colony, and did so on the basis of an authority devolved on them by the representatives of the people.

As such, the new charter government was founded on the basis of the revolutionary principle of popular sovereignty, rather than the sovereignty of the Crown, which represented a critical shift in the locus of 'where sovereignty lay'. The implications of this shift in the locus of sovereign power, however, was somewhat obscured by the town representatives demanding the re-establishment of a government that had been founded originally on the basis of a charter that had been granted by the Crown in the exercise of its sovereign authority.

On June 6th an oath of office was administered to the Governor, Deputy Governor, and Assistants, to govern "according to the Laws of God, and this land", and bear allegiance to King William and Queen Mary. Thereafter, the statutes and laws that had been in effect as of 12 May 1686 were declared in force. The lower Courts were re-established, town meetings were authorized, and all officers of militia holding commissions as of 12 May 1686 were restored to their posts.[48]

As of mid-July 1689 the new government possessed all of the extensive *de facto* powers exercised formerly by the General Court under the Charter of 1629, and its authority rested on the support of the town representatives who maintained that any alteration proposed thereafter by the Crown would have to be ratified by the people.

Although the majority of town representatives who met in Boston held that sovereignty rested with the people, others did not share their belief as to where sovereignty lay. What the new charter government lacked was a recognized legitimacy among all components of the population.

Continuing doubts as to the legitimacy of its authority, and its unsettled status as a self-declared interim government, made it difficult for the revolutionary government to take effective measures against several towns that refused to pay their tax levies, to discipline militia units that refused to march to frontier postings, as well as to deal with disputants who questioned the commissions of the restored Justices of the Peace and the legality of their court rulings.[49]

The legitimacy of the revolutionary government was only firmly established on December 1, 1689 when a letter was received from King William III. The letter, dated August 12, 1689, recognized the revived charter government as a provisional government until such time as the Crown could provide direction concerning the establishment of a more permanent government. It read:

> *"To Such as for the time being take Care of Preserving the Peace and Administering the Laws, in Our Colony of the Massachusetts Bay in New England,*
>
> *Trusty and Welbeloved We greet you well. Whereas Wee are Informed by Several Addresses from our Colony of the Massachusetts Bay, and particularly by the Address coming to us in the name of the Governour, and Council, and Convention of the Representatives of the People of our Said Colony, That you had most Joyfully received the Notice of our Happy Accession to the Throne of these Kingdoms, and Caused the Proclamation thereof to be issued thro'out Our Said Territory.*
>
> *We have therefore thought fitt hereby to Signify Our Royall Aprobation of the Same; and gracious*

Acceptance of Your readiness in performing, what was Necessary on Your parts for the Conservation of the Peace, and Quiet of Our Said Colony.

And Whereas You give us to Understand, that you have taken upon You the Present Care of the Government until you should receive Our Orders therein; We do hereby Authorise and Impower you to Continue in our Name your Care in the Administration thereof, and preservation of the Peace, Until We shall have taken such Resolutions, and given such Direction for the more Orderly Setlement of the Said Government as shall most conduce to Our Service, and the Security, and Satisfaction of our Subjects within that Our Colony.

And so We bid you farewell. Given at Our Court at Whitehall the 12th day of August 1689 In the first Year of our Reign.

By His Majesties Command
Shrewsbury."[50]

The revolutionary popular government had long since taken the form, but not the name, of the former colonial government of the annulled Charter of 1629. Now with the receipt of the Crown's sanction for the continuance in power of the revolutionary government as a provisional government for the Massachusetts Bay Colony, the Governor and Council and Representatives in Convention declared that their government would henceforth be "termed a General Court, and be Accounted such in all Respects".

At the same time the newly-designated General Court appointed three agents to join the Reverend Increase Mather in England to continue negotiations for a restoration of the old Charter.[51] Within days, arrangements were also made to send Sir Edmund Andros and his councillors to England to be indicted for misconduct while in office, on charges brought against them by the new colonial government.[52]

With the receipt of the King's letter, which authorized the revolutionary government to continue in power, there was no doubt remaining as to its legitimacy. The new charter government, which had been established on the basis of popular sovereignty -- the will of the people as expressed through a convention of their elected town representatives -- was empowered to act in the name of Their Majesties in serving as a provisional government.

Although the legitimacy of the revived charter government was highly questionable when it was based solely on the then-novel principle of popular sovereignty, that was no longer the case with the provisional government. It was authorized and empowered by the Crown to govern the colony.

Henceforth, the re-established General Court exercised a recognized sovereignty within the colony, limited only by a self-imposed limitation not to pass any laws contrary to the laws of England in keeping with the terms of the original charter, and a self-professed willingness to accept a future permanent form of government from the Crown, if it met with the approbation of the magistrates and representatives of the General Court.[53]

The members of the re-established General Court pledged allegiance to the King and Queen, and governed the Massachusetts Bay Colony totally independent of the Crown (and Parliament) from the time of the receipt of the King's letter on December 1, 1690, until May 16, 1692. On that date, it was officially superseded by a re-established royal government of the Province of Massachusetts Bay following the arrival from England of a governor appointed by the Crown with a new charter for the colony.[54]

Despite the best efforts of the Massachusetts government's agents negotiating in London, ultimately King William III proved unwilling to grant the Massachusetts Bay Colony a restoration of the Charter of 1629, or a new constitution that would render permanent the colony's interim provisional status as a self-governing sovereign power owing only allegiance to the Crown. Neither sovereign powers, nor sovereignty, would be delegated by the Crown.[55] On October 7, 1691, a new Charter was bestowed by the King. It clearly established the sovereignty of the Crown in the government of a new 'Province of Massachusetts Bay in New England'; yet granted extensive rights and liberties to the colonists.

The Charter of 1691

The Royal Charter of 1691 established the Province of Massachusetts Bay in New England with a General Court form of government, which comprised a Governor and Deputy Governor appointed by the Crown, a Council elected by the Assembly, and an elected Assembly. All public office holders and members of the government were required to swear allegiance to the Crown.

The sovereign power of the Crown was exercised by the Governor, who commanded the militia; had a veto over all legislation, and jurisdiction over the vice-Admiralty courts; and was responsible for the enforcement of colonial trade laws. The Governor also had the right to prorogue and dissolve the General Court at any time; and the Crown possessed a right of disallowance.

All orders, laws, statutes, and ordinances of the General Court, once signed by the Governor, had to be forwarded to England for royal approval. The Crown had a right to void any act of the General Court for a period of up to three years after its submission to the Privy Council. The passage of three years without a disallowance, constituted confirmation by the Crown of any and all acts of the Governor and General Court brought before the Privy Council in that period.

The new royal government established the sovereignty of the Crown beyond dispute, but granted extensive powers to the legislature as well. In addition to the right to elect the Council members and government officials (with the exception of sheriffs, judges, and justices of the peace), the Assembly was to vote the salary of the Governor and public officials; and only the General Court could levy taxes.

Moreover, the Governor could not declare martial law without the Council's consent, nor deploy troops outside the province without the consent of the General Court, or the troops themselves; and the General Court was vested with the right to grant land patents and create townships, thereby resolving a contentious issue. A long standing question, as to whether the English courts had any jurisdiction in the colony, was likewise resolved through a provision that disputants in civil cases of over £300 value had a right of appeal to the Privy Council in England.

The new royal charter of the Province of Massachusetts Bay in New England provided for annual elections; guaranteed the colonists all the rights, liberties, and immunities of Englishmen in the mother country. It also granted freedom of conscience for all Protestants in religious matters, thereby enforcing toleration on the Puritan establishment of the colony, which hitherto had prosecuted, punished, and expelled religious dissenters.

The new Charter also established, for the first time, a broadly-based franchise by granting the vote to 40 shilling freeholders and individuals of £50 net worth. Generally speaking, the new Province Charter was very liberal compared to the terms of the Charter of 1629, and the charters of the royal governments imposed on the other colonies. However, it was designed to assert the absolute sovereignty of the Crown, and to prevent the Massachusetts Bay Colony from re-establishing an independent government.[56]

In an effort to enhance acceptance of the new royal government by the Puritans of the Massachusetts colony, the Crown let the Massachusetts agents in London name the Governor, Deputy Governor, and the first Councillors of the new royal government.

The Reverend Increase Mather did so, and chose mostly members of the existing elected Council of Assistants of the revolutionary provisional government. They were to serve in the new royal government until May 1693 when the Assembly, following new elections, would elect their successors.

The new royal governor, so chosen, was Sir William Phips, the former commander of the Canada expedition of August-November 1690, who was then in London seeking the support of the Crown, gunpowder, ammunition, and the support of Royal Navy frigates, for a second assault against the French in Canada. Phips arrived back in Boston on May 14, 1692, with the Province Charter in hand, to establish the new royal government in which the sovereignty of the Crown was clearly established.[57]

Although the Massachusetts Puritans failed to obtain a restoration of their founding colonial Charter of 1629 (under which the General Court had exercised a *de facto* sovereignty over the territory of the Massachusetts Bay Colony), the General Court of the provisional government acquiesced in the establishment of the new royal provincial government embodying the sovereignty of the Crown. There was no real choice in the spring of 1692.

An on-going costly war with the Wabanaki Indians in Maine, and the devastation inflicted earlier on the frontier settlements by French and Indian marauders following the outbreak of war with France in 1689, had left much of Maine depopulated. A number of towns had been burnt to the ground; over two hundred settlers had been massacred; and much of the population in outlying settlements of the Massachusetts Bay Colony were living in a constant state of fear and alarm. And at sea French privateers were inflicting heavy damage on the coastal trade, the fishery, and ocean commerce.

Within the colony there was once again a shortage of gunpowder and munitions for its defence, which gave rise to fears that France might seek to undertake a sea borne invasion, and land troops in New England. There was little to stop them. The French naval warships were far superior in firepower to the several warships, and armed merchantmen, that New England could command. Moreover, the colony was economically prostrate, and burdened with heavy taxes to pay down an accumulated public debt of £40,000 which had been incurred in defending its frontier settlements and sea coast, and paying for the Phips' Canada Expedition of August-November 1690.

What was perhaps even more distressing for a covenanted people was the "awfull Frown of God" upon them, which they discerned as the principal source of their troubles and afflictions. The visible saints of the General Court saw direct evidence of God's anger, and "the Overruling Providence of God visibly appearing in several Concurrent circumstances to the frustrating of the expedition" to Canada.

The Canada Expedition to their mortification, had been plagued by contrary winds, unseasonable weather, severe storms, outbreaks of smallpox, and a debilitating fever that contributed to the defeat suffered in the attack on Canada and inflicted a heavy loss of life. As such the Governor and Council of the revolutionary-provisional government of the Massachusetts Bay Colony could but pray that:

> *"God grant we may be deeply humbled, and enquire into the cause, and reforme those Sins that have provoked so great Anger to smote against the prayers of his people, and to answer us by terrible things in Righteousness; ...."*[58]

As of the spring of 1692 a further distraction and evidence of the agitated state of mind of a covenanted people suffering numerous afflictions, was the hysteria associated with the Salem witch trials.

During the following summer over 150 women and men were held in jail, while awaiting trial on suspicion of witchcraft, and a further 200 stood accused. The jails were filled, and nineteen persons were executed for witchcraft, and another condemned to death, before the trials were ultimately suspended. It was new Governor, Sir William Phips, who would bring the mania of accusations, imprisonments, interrogations, and executions, of the summer months to an end in October of that year.

A belief in witchcraft, evil spirits, and possession by the devil was but part of the medieval worldview, and during the 16th and 17th centuries both Catholic and Protestant Europe, and to a lesser extent England, experienced great witch hunts and the execution of thousands who were condemned for supposedly practising witchcraft. These hysterical activities were a product of the uncertainties and fears engendered by a rapid growth of population, commercialism, and an emerging individualism, as well as of socio-economic dislocations which were being experienced on the breaking up of the medieval feudal system.

In New England, the dislocations were even more immediate and severe, and the mental anguish exacerbated through the added impact of the several smallpox epidemics, the abject failure and heavy cost of the Canada Expedition, the constant fear and horror of Indian attack, and a prevailing unease that the religious character and zeal of New England Puritanism was fading in the face of commercial development, exposing the colony to further afflictions. To restore the well-being of a covenanted people, action had to be taken to regain God's favour by combatting the devil, and eliminating the evil spirits and witches who were harming Puritan society.[59]

In the face of such distractions and fears, the Puritans of the Massachusetts Bay Colony were in no position to oppose the Crown in a dispute over 'where sovereignty lay', or to resist the imposition of a royal government on the colony. Moreover, for the General Court a major concern, in the year prior to the imposition of the new royal government in May 1692, was the need to secure the support of the English Crown in defending the colony. In particular, the King and Queen were beseeched to provide supplies of gunpowder and munitions, and Royal Navy frigates to protect coastal shipping and the fishery, as well as frigates to support the New Englanders in a contemplated second assault on Canada.

The Puritans remained convinced that only the destruction or subjection of French power in Canada would put an end to the threat of further devastation being visited on New England at the hands of the French and Indians; and that the conquest of Canada, God willing, would require the active support and participation of the Crown.[60] With the very survival of the Massachusetts Bay Colony seemingly at stake, the issue of 'where sovereignty lay' was put in abeyance. Only in cooperating with the Crown in the establishment of the new royal government could New England be relieved of its distracted state.

The Interregnum (April 1689-May 1692)

The establishment of a royal government in the new Province of Massachusetts Bay in May 1692 restored the sovereignty of the Crown over the colony. It brought to an end a three-year interregnum period of political uncertainty that followed on the overthrow of the royal government of the Dominion of New England, on April 18, 1689, upon Bostonians hearing word of the Glorious Revolution in England. During that three-year period, the colony functioned as a *de facto* sovereign state. It was fully self-governing, and owed only a self-professed allegiance to the English Crown.

Between April 1689 and May 1692 the colony was governed by three different forms of government in succession: an *ad hoc*, self-appointed Council for Public Safety; an interim government that mimicked the form of the former charter government, while disclaiming that it was a revived Charter government; and lastly, on June 6, 1689, a new Charter government based on popular sovereignty, which as of December 1, 1689 was approved and empowered by King William to serve as a provisional government until a more permanent government could be established by the Crown.

When formed, in June 1689 in response to the demands of the town representatives, the re-established charter government was totally independent of the Crown, and was a revolutionary popular government. The royal Charter of 1629 no longer existed as a legal document or corporate charter. It had been "annulled, vacated, and annihilated" by a court of law in England. The revived charter government was established by the colonists themselves, based solely on popular sovereignty, the will of the people as expressed by the elected representatives of the towns meeting in a convention. Whatever legitimacy and authority the General Court had when first re-established derived solely from that source.

The new charter government required its member to swear allegiance to the Crown – the new monarchs King William and Queen Mary – but it was a self-professed allegiance; and one of its fundamental principles of the re-established charter government was that no change could be made in the constitution of the government without the expressed consent of the people, conveyed through their elected representatives. In effect, it was a sovereign government.[61]

The inability of the re-established charter government to convince everyone of its legitimacy, however, led the General Court to welcome a communication from King William that authorized and empowered the new charter government to serve as a provisional government until the Crown could re-establish its authority.

In recognizing and empowering the revolutionary popular government the king placed no limits or restrictions on its exercise of the powers, rights, and prerogatives of government within the Massachusetts Bay Colony. In effect, the king's action constituted a bestowal of palatine powers on the re-established General Court government of the colony in return for its pledge of loyalty and allegiance. Strictly speaking, however, it was not a traditional grant of palatine powers as the empowerment of the revolutionary popular government was on a provisional basis, at the pleasure of the king, rather than in perpetuity.

Although the re-established General Court professed a willingness to acquiesce in a future government established by the Crown, there were two unspoken premises: a belief by the members of the General Court that the Charter of 1629 embodied an irrevocable delegation of sovereignty, and would be rightfully restored to them by their Protestant King, William III; and a belief that the people must be consulted on any settlement proposed by the Crown to obtain their approbation. In effect, there was still a dramatic difference between the Crown and the Puritans of the re-established General Court of the Massachusetts Bay Colony as to 'where sovereignty lay'.

Sovereignty and the Canada Expedition

When the Canada Expedition of Sir William Phips was undertaken in August-November 1690, it was during the Interregnum when the provisional government of the Massachusetts Bay Colony, the re-established General Court, enjoyed an absolute power of self-government; and in that capacity was responsible for the defence of the colony.[62]

At that time there was no royal government in the Massachusetts Bay Colony, nor was the English Crown acting in any sovereign capacity within the colony. The General Court was the sovereign power, recognized and empowered by the king, as revealed and conveyed in the letter received nine months earlier in December 1689. Hence, it was the re-established General Court, acting in a sovereign capacity that authorized and undertook the Phips' Canada expedition.

The General Court requisitioned the ships of the fleet, recruited the soldiers, secured the munitions and provisions, financed the enterprise, and appointed and empowered Sir William Phips to command the expedition. Moreover, although the expedition was initiated, authorized, and conducted, totally independent of the Crown, without any royal sanction or support; all of the actions taken were deemed to be "for their Majesties Service", and were undertaken in the name of their Majesties King William and Queen Mary, in recognition of the General Court's self-professed loyalty and allegiance to the Crown.[63]

For the participants in the Phips' Canada Expedition it was clear 'where sovereignty lay' as evidenced in the orders given to Sir William Phips on his appointment to command, by the Articles of War, which governed the conduct of the troops, and the terms of the surrender ultimatum presented to the French.

On his appointment as General of all the Forces on July 4, 1690, Sir William Phips was ordered to conduct his forces:

> *"According to the Rules, and Discipline of Warr, and Yourself to Observe, and Obey all such Orders, and Instructions as You shall receive from the Governour, and Council, or General Court of this Colony for their Majesties Service."*

On September 23, 1690, while the invasion fleet commanded by Phips was at anchor at Tadoussac in the lower St. Lawrence River, a Council of War was held and Articles of War circulated to each ship. The 23 Articles of War set forth the laws and ordinances that would govern the conduct and discipline of the soldiers, and sailors, and ships, during the pending battle, and the treatment of prisoners, women and children, and enemy property, as well as the seizure of plunder.

The first article clearly established that the New England fleet and soldiers, although serving in the name of the Crown, were acting under the authority of the government of the Massachusetts Bay colony, the re-established General Court, and were subject only to the laws and ordinances of that government.

> "Order: 1 That the laws and ordinances of war passed by the General Court of the Massachusetts, for the better regulating their forces; together with all such additional laws and orders as shall now be made and ordained by this Council at their present session; be forthwith read and published at the head of each regiment or company of souldiers, and on board each and every ship and vessel in their Majesties Service for this present expedition to Canada, etc. And that the same be put in execution according to the true intend and meaning thereof." [64]

On anchoring opposite Quebec, on October 6th, Sir William Phips issued an ultimatum, under a white flag, that demanded that the French surrender "in the Name and in the Behalf of Their Most Excellent Majesties, William and Mary, King and Queen of England, Scotland, France and Ireland, Defenders of the Faith, and By Order of Their said Majesties Government of the Massachusetts-Colony in New-England".[65]

In sum, the surrender was ordered by the Government of the Massachusetts Bay Colony, a revolutionary provisional government that had been authorized and empowered to govern in the name of the Crown. Hence, the wording of the surrender ultimatum demanded that the French surrender in the name of, and on behalf of, Their Majesties King William and Queen Mary, but by order of the Government of the Massachusetts Bay Colony, the sovereign power under whose authority the expedition was authorized and undertaken.

Conclusion

From the founding of the Massachusetts Bay plantation by the royal Charter of 1629, the Puritans of the Massachusetts Bay Colony continually strove to establish a sovereign government in the colony, while professing loyalty and allegiance to the Crown. In effect they sought to establish a relationship analogous to that of a vassal-in-chief enjoying palatine powers embodied in the exercise of sovereignty over the colony with only an allegiance owed to the Crown in an age when sovereignty was divisible. That effort resulted in an on-going struggle throughout the 17th Century over 'where sovereignty lay', which waxed and waned according to political developments in England.

There were periods when the charter government exercised a *de facto* sovereignty over the Massachusetts Bay Colony territory unlimited by the Crown, such as during the English Civil War and Cromwell era, and there were other periods when the sovereignty of the Crown was clearly established through the imposition of a royal government, such as under James II (1686) and William III (1692). However, at the time of the Phips' Canada Expedition in the late summer and fall of 1690, there was no doubt 'where sovereignty lay'.

Recognized and empowered by the Crown, the revolutionary popular government of the re-established General Court exercised an unchallenged sovereignty in the Massachusetts Bay Colony from December 1, 1689 through to May 16, 1692, when it was superseded by the imposition of a new royal government. During that interregnum period, both the Crown and the Puritan colonists recognized the sovereignty of the General Court over the Massachusetts Bay Colony, but continued to differ over 'where sovereignty lay' ultimately.

From the viewpoint of the Crown, sovereignty was divisible and royal powers – palatine powers – could be granted or delegated to an individual, or group of individuals, to hold and govern a specified territory within the king's realm in return for the performance of specified duties, and allegiance to the Crown. However, the founding Charter of 1629 of the Massachusetts Bay Colony did not bestow a grant of sovereignty.

It was simply a corporate charter that delegated local government and magisterial functions to the trading company over its territory, the settlement on Massachusetts Bay. Moreover, ultimately the Massachusetts Bay Charter of 1629 had been declared null and void by the courts in England on the grounds that the king had been deceived in his grant. Hence, sovereignty resided indisputably in the Crown.

In contrast, the Massachusetts Puritans maintained that sovereignty resided permanently in their General Court government; although not all colonists were in agreement as to the source of that sovereign power.[66] Some held that the people were sovereign. This was the position of the elected representatives from the country towns in the Convention of May 1689 who insisted that the charter government be revived according to the will of the people; and that the revived charter government could not be changed without the consent of the elected representatives of the people.

Others recognized the King as the Dominion Sovereign, but claimed that the Crown had granted sovereignty over the Massachusetts Bay Colony territory in perpetuity to the Massachusetts Bay Company proprietors, or 'freemen' of the colony, in the Charter of 1629. In effect, it was maintained that the granting of a trading company charter, which had delegated wide powers of local government, constituted a grant of palatine powers over the territory of the Massachusetts Bay Colony. This later view was championed by the leaders of the re-established General Court government who expected that the Charter of 1629 would be restored to them by the new Protestant King, William III.

Regardless of internal differences of belief concerning how sovereignty was bestowed on the General Court, the Massachusetts Puritans were united in their belief that their charter government was a sovereign power, owing only loyalty and allegiance to the Crown.

For the Puritans of the Massachusetts Bay Colony their interpretation of, and actions in defence of, the Charter of 1629 were a product of the Puritan mind, their religious worldview derived from their Calvinist theology. They had come to the New World to put their scriptural beliefs into practice by establishing, on Massachusetts Bay, a religious settlement governed by the saints gathered together in a Covenant of Grace directly under God, the absolute sovereign of the universe. Their community was a theocracy, governed by the laws of Scripture, not the laws of man; and it was conceived as a "City upon a Hill", a shining example of a religious community established and prospering under Providence in the service of God.

It is a decidedly moot point as to whether the Massachusetts Bay Puritans believed that the Hand of God had guided the hand of Charles II in granting their founding Charter, but there is no doubt that the Puritan interpretation of the Charter of 1629 was that it bestowed upon them, and indeed could not but have conveyed to them, an irrevocable grant of sovereignty.

To the Puritans it was, in effect, a grant of palatine powers, with the government of the colony to be exercised by the General Court, the representative embodiment of God's chosen people, independent of any external authority. How could the "City upon a Hill" be governed by God's laws if it was subject to the dictates of an earthy sovereign? Within the Puritan religious worldview to do God's work and live according to God's Word, His chosen people had to be autonomous and free of any external temporal rule and corruption; and God, who ordained whatever came to pass under His Divine Providence, would not have had let it be otherwise.

Viewed from such a bias of mind, the whole legal concept of a corporate charter, and what it actually conveyed, was meaningless. The Puritans interpreted their founding charter, and what it bestowed on the Massachusetts Bay Company, from within their own particular theology and religious worldview, and their actions in defence of the charter were based on, and motivated by, their particular mind set.

Moreover, the Puritans of the Massachusetts Bay Colony

identified directly with, and saw themselves as part of international Calvinism, and felt the oppression visited upon their brethren in England under the Stuart restoration after 1660. The Boston insurrection of 1689 was as much a product of their fears of what had befallen Calvinists (Presbyterians) in England, and their perceived need to regain control over the 'City upon a Hill' through restoring their theocratic government, as it was a reaction against the government of Sir Edmund Andros. The arrival of the Prince of Orange in England, and his pronouncements, were simply a catalyst for action. [67]

Although the Puritans of the Massachusetts Bay Colony and the Crown held diverging views as to 'where sovereignty lay', conflict was avoided during the Interregnum (April 1689-May 1692) by the adroit manoeuvre of King William III in authorizing and empowering the revolutionary popular government to continue to govern the colony as a provisional government, with the authority to act in the Name of, and on behalf of, the Crown during a time of crisis in the colony and in Europe.

When the Crown ultimately sought to re-assert sovereignty over the Massachusetts Bay Colony by re-establishing a royal government, conflict was avoided, in the spring of 1692, through the conciliatory actions of the Crown. Extensive powers were given to the legislature in the new royal government, and leading members of the last elected charter government of May 1686 – most of whom were leading members of the revolutionary provisional government – were appointed to the executive of the new royal government, as well as to the positions of Governor and Deputy Governor.

Moreover, at that time the Massachusetts Bay Colony was prostrate both economically and militarily, and was in an agitated state of mind in suffering under numerous afflictions amidst the distractions leading up to the Salem witch trials. As such the revolutionary popular government was in no position to actively resist any exercise of royal authority. Hence, the elected representatives of the people acquiesced in the new royal government, which embodied the sovereignty of the Crown over the Massachusetts Bay Colony, and an open conflict with the Crown over 'where sovereignty lay' was avoided, or at least postponed.

Whatever the belief of the various parties as to 'where sovereignty lay', all were agreed that the re-established General Court held sovereignty over the Massachusetts Bay Colony territory during the period, from December 1689 through May 1692 – the period following the receipt of the King's letter authorizing and empowering the revolutionary popular government to govern as a provisional government in the Name of and on behalf of the Crown.

During that period all government acts, appointments and laws, were authorized and enforced solely on the sovereign authority of the re-established General Court, but promulgated in the name of Their Majesties, King William and Queen Mary.

Where the Phips' Canada Expedition of 1690 was concerned, all of the acts authorizing and governing the undertaking of that venture were issued and enforced by order of the sovereign authority of the General Court of the Massachusetts Bay Colony, but were promulgated in the name of Their Majesties, King William and Queen Mary, in Their Majesties' Service.

At that time the re-established General Court of the Massachusetts Bay Colony was a sovereign power that owed only loyalty and allegiance to the Crown in whose name and on behalf of whom it governed. In sum, the palatine power status enjoyed by the Massachusetts Bay Colony accounts for the seemingly contradictory wording of the surrender ultimatum presented to Count Frontenac, the Governor General of New France, by Sir William Phips at Quebec in October 1690.

1. Text of Phips' ultimatum, printed in Cotton Mather, *The Life of Sir William Phips*, Mark Van Doren, ed. (New York: AMS Press, 1919, 1st. ed. 1797), pp. 73-74. The term 'palatine' means 'of the palace', and conveys that the vassal-in-chief held royal powers over his territory directly from the king.

2. George H. Sabine, *A History of Political Theory*, 3rd. ed. (New York: Holt, Rineholt & Winston, 1961), pp. 405-408.

3. See, for example, the Charter of Maryland, June 20, 1632, and the Charter of Carolina, March 24, 1663, and of June 30, 1665, as elaborated upon in this chapter.

4. William Stubbs, *The Constitutional History of England in its Origin and Development*, vol. III (Oxford: Clarendon Press, 1878), pp. 558-587, "Growth of the Corporation".

5. See, for example, the Charter of Massachusetts Bay, March 4, 1629, and its annulment, as examined in this chapter.

6. Quoted by Edmund S. Morgan, *The Puritan Dilemma, The Story of John Winthrop*, ed. by Oscar Handlin, (Boston: Little, Brown and Company, 1958), pp. 84-85.

7. Morgan, *Puritan Dilemma*, pp. 85 & 168.

8. Paul Johnson, *A History of the American People* (London: Orion Books, 1998), pp. 31-47; and Perry Miller, *The New England Mind: From Colony to Province* (Cambridge, Mass.: Harvard University Press, 1962), pp. 21-26. On the Puritan theory of state and concepts of fundamental law, the covenant, and the congregational system, see Perry Miller, *ibid*, and Thomas H. Johnson, *The Puritans* (New York: American Book Company, 1938), pp. 101-192; and *Encylopaedia Britannica*, 15th ed., Vol. 15 (1980), "Puritanism", pp. 304-308, and *ibid*, vol. 4 (1980), "Congregationalists", pp. 1127-1130. See also John von Rohr, *The Covenent of Grace in Puritan Thought* (Atlanta, Georgia: Scholars Press, 1986), esp. pp. 135-153, on the 17th century Puritans beliefs.

Arminianism was named after James Arminius (1560-1609), a theologian of the Dutch Reformed Church, who rejected the Calvinist doctrine of absolute predestination in favour of free will. The purging of Puritan clergy from the Anglican Church was carried out under William Laud (Bishop of London, 1628-1633, Archbishop of Canterbury, 1633-1640). See Charles Carlton, *Archbishop William Laud* (London: Rutledge & Kegan Paul, 1987), pp. 1-204). For a brief discussion of Arminianism, and its impact on the Anglican Church, see *ibid*, pp. 11-13.

9. Miller, *Colony to Province*, pp. 6-7. The year 1629, when the Puritans left England to found the Massachusetts Bay Colony, was a black year for Protestantism. In the religious wars in Europe the Catholic powers achieved a series of major military victories in suppressing their Protestant subjects, in conquering and forcibly reconverting Protestant principalities, free towns, and ecclesiastical lands, and in advancing the establishment of monarchical absolutism within each sovereign Catholic state under a single state religion, Roman Catholicism.

In the lowlands, Catholic Spain under Philip IV laid siege to the Calvinist Dutch republic; in France Louis XIII and Cardinal Richelieu destroyed the military power of the Calvinist Huguenots; in Austria and Bohemia Protestant subjects were forcibly reconverted or expelled; and in Germany, where the Thirty Year's War (1618-1648) raged, the Catholic Emperor Ferdinand II of the Austrian Hapsburgs, with the aid of the Spanish Hapsburgs, inflicted crushing defeats on the Protestant princes and their ally, Lutheran Denmark. Moreover, England was forced to sue for peace with Spain in 1629 and with France in 1630, abandoning the Protestant cause.

10. Thomas Hutchinson, *The History of the Colony and Province of Massachusetts-bay*, ed. Lawrence Shaw Mayo (Cambridge: Massachusetts-Harvard University Press, 1936), pp. 367-383; and Morgan, *Puritan Dilemma*, pp. 89-112, and 157-160.

11. Attorney Thomas Lechford, 1642, quoted in Hutchinson, *History of the Colony*, p. 380. In England the star-chamber was abolished in 1641.

12. Michael G. Hall, Lawrence H. Leder, and Michael G. Kammen, eds., *The Glorious Revolution in America: Documents on the Colonial Crisis of 1689* (Chapel Hill: University of North Carolina Press, 1964), p. 10; and Morgan, *Puritan Dilemma*, p. 196. From the time of the removal of the Massachusetts Bay Company from England there had been concerns that the Puritans were bent on seceding and establishing a sovereign power in the new world. (See George L. Beer, *The Origins of the British Colonial System, 1578-1660* (New York: Macmillan Company, 1922), pp. 25-28).

In England the new concept of absolute sovereignty gave birth at the beginning of the 17th Century to a long struggle over 'where sovereignty lay'. It eventually pitted royalists who argued for the absolute sovereignty of the Crown (in maintaining that the King was an absolute monarch under God and Parliament only an advisory body), against parliamentarians who championed parliamentary sovereignty focussing on the 'King in Parliament' with the king governing with the consent of Parliament.

The parliamentary struggle was led by mercantile interests who wanted to protect property, end royal trade monopolies, and control taxes and trade regulations, and by the Puritans who wanted to reform the established Church of England, and to align England with the Calvinist Netherlands and the Protestant Princes of Germany against Catholic Spain and the Catholic Emperor of the Holy Roman Empire (the German Reich).   See George L. Mosse, *The Struggle for Sovereignty in England, From the Reign of Queen Elizabeth to the Petition of Right* (New York: Octagon Books, 1950, reprinted 1968).

In England, however, the theory of divine right of kings failed to buttress the king's claim. Both the theory, and its corollary the duty of the subject to yield an absolute and passive obedience to the king, had little real political impact despite the espousal of the theory by James I at an early date in his *Trew Law of Free Monarchies* (1598). See Sabine, *Political Theory*, pp. 391-397, & 442.

13. *Encylopaedia Britannica*, 15th. ed., vol. 15 (1980), "Puritanism", p. 306 . Earlier under the Protectorate of Oliver Cromwell, Laudian Anglican clergy were purged from their livings; whereas under the Stuart Restoration steps were taken to purge the Presbyterian

(Calvinist) clergy from the established Church of England, in turn. There were four major acts of the 'Cavalier" Parliament, referred to collectively as the Clarendon Code, that were enacted to exclude Calvinists (Presbyterians), as well as other Nonconformists, from the established Church, the universities, and government, following on the restoration of the Stuarts. They were:

The *Corporation Act* (December 1661), which prescribed that, in addition to taking the Oath of Allegiance, an individual to be eligible for election to a city government or corporation must be in communion with the established Church of England, and must take the Oath of Supremacy, which involved testifying to and recognizing the monarch as the head of the established Church, as well as head of State;

The *Act of Uniformity* (May 1662), which prescribed that the administration of the sacraments, and the liturgy, rites and doctrines of the established Church of England must be in conformity with The Book of Common Prayer; that to hold and administer a parish the minister must have received an episcopal ordination; and that lecturers and teachers to hold their position must be in communion with the established Church of England and take an Oath denouncing the Solemn League and Covenant of 1642, whereby English Presbyterians during the Civil War had vowed to reform the Anglican Church and establish a Presbyterian system of church government;

The *Conventicle Act* (1664), which prescribed a punishment at law for anyone over 16 years of age who attended a religious meeting of more than five persons that was not conducted according to The Book of Common Prayer; and

The *Five Mile Act* (1665), which forbade expelled Presbyterian ministers from living within five miles of their former parish, and which required lecturers and teachers to swear allegiance to the king, to conform to the liturgy of the Church of England in their teachings, and to take an oath denouncing the Solemn League and Covenant (1642).

It was the rigid enforcement of the Corporation Act and the Act of Uniformity by Charles II that drove the English Presbyterian clergy – some 2,000 Calvinists ministers – out of the Church of England in what was denoted as "The Great Ejection". The enforcement of the Five Mile Act resulted in covenanted congregations going five miles out of their parish to attend services and hear sermons from their former minister, which presented a problem of maintaining public order to any local official seeking to enforce the Conventicle Act.

The Puritans of New England were also, in effect, expelled from the Church of England by the Clarendon Code acts in being branded as nonconformists for their Calvinistic beliefs; although the acts did not apply to the North American colonies. The colonial charter governments (both palatine and corporate) were not subject to English laws; although corporate charter governments were bound not to pass any laws contrary to the laws of England. Moreover, in the colonies dissenters formed the majority of the population in the 17th Century. (In England, the Conventicle Act and the Five Mile Act were repealed in 1689 by parliament under the new monarchs, King William and Queen Mary; and parliament passed the Act of Toleration in May 1689 allowing freedom of worship to nonconformists on taking the Oath of Allegiance and Oath of Supremacy.)

14. Miller, *Colony to Province*, pp. 10-11. The Westminster Confession of 1646 was prepared by English divines at the instigation of the Long Parliament during the English Civil War. The confession expressed an adherence to Calvinist theology, including the doctrine of predestination, and became the statement of faith of English Presbyterians. It was adopted by the Church of Scotland in 1647, and approved by Parliament in June 1648 for England, but never enforced. The Separatists, or Independents, were Puritans who had separated from the Church of England to form independent congregations based on the Covenant of Grace and Puritan doctrines.

15. The Puritans of the Massachusetts Bay Colony, however, did not withdraw immediately from the Church of England. They continued during the 1640s to profess the Thirty-nine Articles of the Anglican Church, and saw themselves as part of the national communion and apostolic succession though not through the laying on of hands. The Westminster Confession and the Cambridge Platform were regarded as elaborations on existing doctrines that further 'purified' or reformed the national Church of England. Only towards the end of the century did they begin to refer to themselves as Congregationalists, independent of

the Church of England (Miller, *Colony to Province*, p. 464).

16. Richard R. Johnson, *Adjustment to Empire, The New England Colonies, 1675-1715* (New Brunswick, New Jersey: Rutgers University Press, 1981), p. 41; and Morgan, *Puritan Dilemma*, p. 196.

17. "The General Court Reports on Massachusetts' Allegiance to the Crown", June 10, 1661, printed in Hall, Leder, and Kammen, eds., *Documents on the Colonial Crisis*, pp. 12-13.

18. Hutchinson, *History of the Colony*, pp. 367-385.

19. Beer, *The Origins of the British Colonial System*, pp. 320 and 326.

20. The granting of palatine powers, or sovereignty over a particular territory, to a vassal-in-chief by the king in return for allegiance (primarily a specified duty of military service), was a medieval feudal land tenure concept imported into England from France.

In England under King William I, following the Norman Conquest of 1066, there were four palatine counties established to defend invasion routes: the Bishopric of Durham (Scottish border); the Bishopric of Kent (cross Channel invasion); and the earldoms of Chester and Shropshire (Welsh marches). In the palatinate of Chester, for example, the Earl held all lands (non-ecclesiastical), had his own courts, issued his own writs, appointed the judges and peace officers, held his own parliament (attended by the barons of his territory), levied taxes, and controlled his own military forces. He was a feudal sovereign in his own domain governing independent of the king; yet he owed allegiance and fealty to the king, who granted the palatine powers under the medieval concept of divisible sovereignty. The Earl was bound by his oath of allegiance to protect the King's lands and honour against his enemies "both within England and without".

More generally feudalism was 'a perpetual right in a piece of land that is the property of another', and each property holder swore allegiance to, and owed service to, the liege lord from whom he held the land with only the vassal-in-chief swearing allegiance to, and owing service to, the king. However, in England William I retained the Saxon system, or German variant on the feudal system, wherein all property holding vassals swore allegiance directly to the king and owed military service directly to the king. (See William Stubbs, *The Constitutional History of England, In Its Origin and Development*, Vol. I (New York: Barnes & Noble, 6th ed., 1967, 1st. ed., 1897), pp. 293-295, 392-395, and 273-291.

21. Historically, with the exception of Rhode Island and Connecticut, each of the thirteen colonies came at various times under different forms of government – charter, proprietary and/or royal – in the period from their founding to the American Revolution. The Maryland Charter of 1632 and the Carolina Charter of 1663 are examined herein simply to explain and illustrate, through two historical examples, the scope and nature of the palatine powers bestowed through a Dominion Sovereign granting a charter conveying sovereignty over a territory, as distinct from the limited and circumscribed governing powers granted in a corporate charter to a trading company over a particular territory for trade and local government purposes.

22. "The Maryland Charter, 1632", Yale University Law School Avalon Project, http:/www.yale.edu/lawweb /avalon/states/ma01.htm. The Maryland proprietor and the Carolina proprietors were also granted the right to create a landed aristocracy of barons through granting lands in feudal tenure, as well as the right to establish a Baron-court or governing council of barons. This right, however, remained a dead letter both in Maryland and Carolina.

23. "Charter of Carolina - March 24, 1663, and "Charter of Carolina - June 30, 1665", Yale University Law School Avalon Project, http:/www.yale.edu/lawweb/avalon/states/nc01.htm, and *ibid*, /nc04.htm. The Carolina Charters of 1663 and 1665 broke new ground, however, in that the Crown gave the proprietors the right to grant liberty of conscience and toleration to inhabitants who "for conscience sake" could not conform to the liturgy, ceremonies, oaths and articles of the national Church, so that they might not be disturbed in their peace and safety so long as they did not disturb the peace or "reproach the said liturgy, forms and ceremonies" of the said Church of England (*ibid*). However, in New England a parallel effort by the Crown to promote the toleration of Protestant religious dissenters met with resistance from the Puritans who continued to persecute Quakers and Antinomians

in the Massachusetts Bay Colony. (See Perry Miller, *From Colony to Province*, pp. 126-127).

24. There were at least two legal grounds on which the Crown could seek annulment of a patent, or corporate charter, before the higher courts: viz. that the proprietor or corporation had exceeded the liberties granted in the charter (writ of *quo warranto*), or that the king had been deceived in his grant (writ of *scire facias*). See below in text.

25. "The King's Instructions to the Royal Commissioners appointed to entreat with the New England Colonies", April 23, 1664, in Hall, Leder, and Kammen, eds., *Documents on the Colonial Crisis*, pp. 14-18.

26. R. Johnson, *Adjustment to Empire*, pp. 27-28 & 36-37; David S. Lovejoy, *The Glorious Revolution in America* (New York: Harper & Row Publishers, 1972), pp. 131-143; and Philip S. Haffenden, "The Crown and the Colonial Charters, 1675-1688", *William and Mary Quarterly*, XIV, Part I (July 1958), pp. 297-311, and Part II (October 1958), pp. 452-466. See also Edward Randolph, "A Short narrative touching the delivery of your Majesties letters to the Magistrates of Boston in New England", September 20, 1676, in Hall, Leder, & Kammen, eds., *Documents on the Colonial Crisis*, pp. 18-19.

The Navigation Acts of 1651, 1660, 1663, and 1664, were designed to strength English shipping and focus imperial trade on the mother country. They required that the export trade be carried in English or colonial ships; that the import trade be carried in English ships, colonial ships, or a ship of the country of origin; that all ships bound for the colonies must stop in an English port and pay customs duties; and that certain enumerated colonial goods, such as sugar, indigo, and cotton, be shipped only to England for sale.

27. Theodore B. Lewis jr., "Massachusetts and the Glorious Revolution, 1660-1692" (Ph.D. diss., University of Wisconsin, 1967), pp. 123-145. See also Hall, Leder, & Kammen, eds., *Documents*, pp. 18-19 & 24-25, "The Grounds for Revoking the Colonial Charter", June 4, 1683.

28. Michael G. Hall, *The Last American Puritan: the life of Increase*

Mather, 1639-1723 (Middleton, Connecticut: Wesleyan University Press, 1988), p. 203; and Lovejoy, *The Glorious Revolution*, p. 159.

29. Hall, Leder, & Kammen, eds., *Documents on the Colonial Crisis*, pp. 25-27, "Sir Edmund Andros' Commission as Governor", April 7, 1686. See also Lovejoy, *Glorious Revolution*, pp. 125-140 & 168-170; Johnson, *Adjustment to Empire*, pp. 40-63; and Haffenden, "The Crown and the Colonial Charters, 1675-1688", Part I, pp. 297-311, and Part II, pp. 452-466. The efforts of James II to assert the sovereignty of the English Crown were but a pale imitation of the absolute monarchies established in France, under Louis XIII and Louis XIV, and elsewhere in Europe during the 17th Century. In France the concept of absolute sovereignty, as initially expounded by a leading French jurist, Jean Bodin, *Six Livres de la républic* (1576), and the divine right theory on the source of a ruler's sovereign power, as enunciated by Pierre de Belloy, *De l'authorité du roi* (1588), together provided a strong theoretical basis for monarchical absolutism.

The theory of absolute sovereignty was a secularization, and application to individual states, of a hitherto novel papal concept of "plenitudo potentatis" first enunciated by Pope Innocent IV, and confirmed as Church doctrine by Pope Boniface VIII in the bull *Unam sanctam* (1302). In breaking with the medieval tradition of limited and delegated powers, and established contractual rights of the feudal land tenure system, the papacy claimed to possess a supreme power that was absolute, indefeasible, and sovereign over both the ecclesiastical and temporal realms.

It amounted to a claim of universal sovereignty under God based on the grounds that Jesus Christ had invested his disciple Peter, and Peter's successors as the vicar of Christ in Rome (the Pope), with supreme authority from God to validate and enforce (with the sword of the temporal authorities) all human laws, and to command an absolute obedience from all ecclesiastics, temporal rulers, and subjects in Christendom. (Sabine, *Political Theory*, pp. 272-273).

30. Lewis, "Massachusetts and the Glorious Revolution", pp. 213-219, 227-228, & 247-278. The legality of land grants made by towns incorporated by authority of the General Court was questioned by the Andros government. Under English law a corporation could not create

a corporation, and the General Court was legally a corporation, not a sovereign power. Hence the landowners were required to petition the Royal Government for confirmation of their land titles, and had to pay fees for the transaction as well as an annual quit rent on the land (Hall, *The Last American Puritan*, p. 207.) On the revolution in England see: Lucille Pinkham, *William III and the Respectable Revolution* (Cambridge: Harvard University Press, 1954), pp. 72-151; and J.R. Jones, *The Revolution of 1688 in England* (London: Weidenfeld & Nicolson, 1972), pp. 288-316.

31. Accounts of the insurrection of April 18th can be found in: Hutchinson, *History of the Colony*, pp. 317-323; Johnson, *Adjustment to Empire*, pp. 84-95; Lovejoy, *Glorious Revolution*, pp. 226-227 & 240-241; Lewis, "Massachusetts and the Glorious Revolution", pp. 300-315; and Richard R. Johnson, *John Nelson, Merchant Adventurer, A Life Between Empires* (London: Oxford University Press, 1991), pp. 50-54.

32. "The Declaration of the Gentlemen, Merchants, and Inhabitants of Boston, and the Country Adjacent", April 18, 1690, in Robert Earle Moody & Richard Clive Simmons, eds., *The Glorious Revolution in Massachusetts, Selected Documents* (Boston: The Colonial Society of Massachusetts, 1988), pp. 45-51.

33. "A Council for the Safety of the People and Conservation of Peace", April 20, 1689, in Moody & Simmons, *Selected Documents*, p. 54, and Council of Safety orders of April 20th & April 22nd-23rd, in *ibid*, pp. 55-59. A further 22 prominent citizens were soon added to the Council, which ultimately totalled 37 members. On the leading role played by the Boston merchants, and in particular John Nelson, in the insurrection of April 1689, see Richard R. Johnson, *John Nelson Merchant Adventurer, A Life Between Empires* (New York/Oxford: Oxford University Press, 1991), pp. 49-55.

34. On Mather's efforts in England, see Moody, *Selected Documents*, "Introduction", pp. 16f.; and Lovejoy, *The Glorious Revolution in America*, pp. 227-231.

35. "Copy of Act of Council for Safety", 2 May 1689, in Moody &

Simmons, *Selected Documents*, pp. 361-362.

36. Declaration voted at the Chamber of the Country Representatives, May 10, 1689, in Moody & Simmons, *Selected Documents*, p. 71. See also Johnson, *Adjustment to Empire*, pp. 100-103.

37. See reply of Council for Safety, May 10, 1689, and the subsequent declaration of the representatives, May 10, 1689, in Moody & Simmons, *Selected Documents*, pp. 71-73.

38. "To the Kings and Queen's Most Excellent Majesties", 20 May 1689, in Moody & Simmons, *Selected Documents*, pp. 77-78.

39. Miller, *The New England Mind: From Colony to Province*, pp. 130, 158-160. As of 1688 Catholic France, with a large standing royal army under an absolute monarch, Louis XIV, was the most feared and powerful nation in Europe. For several decades absolutist France had waged wars of conquest against both its Protestant and Catholic neighbours, and had suppressed Protestantism both in France and in its conquered territories.

Earlier, in 1685 the persecution of French Calvinist Huguenots had intensified with the revocation of the Edict of Nantes that had guaranteed their political and religious liberties in France; the Protestant Rhineland (the Palatinate) was conquered by France and subjected to a deliberate policy of plunder and devastation; and in England James II, a fervent Catholic, ascended the throne amidst fears that he intended to convert England to Catholicism with the aid of French money and arms. (See David Ogg, *Louis XIV*, 2nd. ed. (London: Oxford University Press, 1967), pp. 47-80.)

The religious wars of the early 17th Century had concluded with the Peace of Westphalia (1648) that recognized the independence of the Calvinist Dutch Republic (the new United Provinces of the Netherlands) and the Swiss Cantons; and established the Protestant and Catholic Principalities and Free Cities of Germany as palatine powers, or sovereign powers, owing allegiance to the Catholic Emperor. As such the Electors and Princes were absolute sovereigns empowered to govern their territories independent of any outside authority, with the authority to make war, conclude alliances, and treat for peace. As vassals granted a fiefdom by the Emperor, the duty of allegiance owed by the Princes was that they were not to enter into alliances against the Emperor, or to aid the enemy of the Emperor, or to let enemies of the Emperor pass through their territory unopposed; and both parties were bound to maintain "a reciprocal amity". (http://tufts.edu/departments, "Treaty of Westphalia, Munster, October 24, 1648", text of treaty, clauses IV, V, XXIII, LXIV, and LXV).

In the treaty the older principle of "cujus regio egus religio" (the Prince's religion is the state religion) was confirmed and extended to embrace Calvinists, in addition to Lutherans and Catholics, and religious toleration was established within the Empire by granting religious minorities a right to private worship, religious education, equality in civic life, and the liberty to sell their property and emigrate. See ibid, clause XLIX; and Leo Gross, "The Peace of Westphalia, 1648-1948", in Charlotte Ku and Paul F. Diehl, eds., *International Law, Classic and Contemporary Readings* (Boulder, Colorado: Lynne Reinner Publishers Inc., 1998), pp. 57-58.

Religious toleration, however, was not practised by the Catholic power signatories within their own countries where the Catholic Counter-Reformation was in full force, or in their territories and colonies. Moreover, Pope Innocent X denounced any agreement with the Protestants. Hence the continuing fears of the New England Puritans, particularly in the face of the later persecutions and ravages of Louis XIV, that the Pope and the Catholic powers were bent on extirpating the Protestant religion.

40. Hutchinson, *History of the Colony*, p. 328; and J.R. Jones, *The Revolution of 1688 in England* (London: Weidenfeld & Nicolson, 1972), pp. 312-316.

41. Hutchinson, *History of the Colony*, p. 329.

42. Returns of Town Meetings received by the Council of Safety during May 1689, in Moody & Simmons, *Selected Documents*, pp. 360-391; and R. Johnson, *Adjustment to Empire*, pp. 105-107.

43. Public Record Office, Colonial Office, 5:855, 44-45, "At a Convention of the Representatives of the several Towns and Villages of

the Massachusetts Colony in New England", 24 May 1689, in Moody & Simmons, *Selected Documents*, pp. 392-395. In the 17th Century, in disputes over 'where sovereignty lay', all parties believed that God was the ultimate absolute sovereign. The argument was over who embodied that sovereign authority here on earth – the King (God's anointed), the Pope (the vicar of Christ), or the people of a nation (God's people), and the arguments took various forms depending on the nature of the contending parties in any particular country or state.

44. It is not surprising that the Puritans evolved a belief in popular sovereignty given their doctrine of the Covenant, and belief that the Christian fellowship of a congregation should elect and ordain its own minister, and establish the terms of the minister's contract. As early as May 1638, a dissenting minister, Thomas Hooker, preached a sermon at Hartford on the Connecticut River, "stating that all authority, in state or religion, must rest on the people's consent". (Johnson, *A History of the American People*, p. 55).

In England popular sovereignty was not set forth as a basis for legitimizing a government during the Convention Parliament that bestowed the throne on King William and Queen Mary (see R. Johnson, *Adjustment to Empire*, p. 102, fn. 75). However, it was a radical party of Independents (Calvinist Congregationalists), the so-called Levellers within Cromwell's army, who first enunciated the theory of popular sovereignty as early as 1648 during the English Civil War. For the Levellers the people were sovereign; Parliament exercised an authority delegated by the people; and laws were valid and binding only if they received the consent of the people as expressed through their elected representatives. Moreover, the Levellers held that all men were born equal, and espoused either universal manhood suffrage (excluding paupers) or a very low property qualification for enfranchisement.

The Levellers, who were precursors of later radical democrats, also put forth a then-novel interpretation of natural law in maintaining that all men were endowed by Nature with innate and inalienable rights to liberty and freedom which the political and legal institutions were established to protect (Sabine, *Political Theory*, pp. 482-489). The New England Puritans were far from being democrats or egalitarians, but the concept of popular sovereignty was a logical extension of their religious beliefs with ' the people' identified as the members of their national covenant.

45. Public Record Office, Colonial Office, 5:855, no. 17, "Paper presented to the Town Representatives", 24 May 1689, in Moody & Simmons, *Selected Documents*, pp. 82-83.

46. Moody & Simmons, *Selected Documents*, "Introduction", pp. 7-10.

47. "The Declaration of the Representatives of the Several Towns in the Massachusetts Colony", June 7, 1689, in Moody & Simmons, *Selected Documents*, pp. 90-91; and Hutchinson, *History of the Colony*, pp. 328-329.

48. Theodore B. Lewis jr., "Massachusetts and the Glorious Revolution, 1660-1692" (Ph.D. diss., University of Wisconsin, 1967), pp. 332-334; and Declarations of the Governor and Council and the Convention of Representatives of the People, June 6th, June 22nd, and July 4th, 1689, in Moody & Simmons, *Selected Documents*, pp. 88-92, 108, & 120-121.

49. Lewis, "Massachusetts and the Glorious Revolution", pp. 340-343.

50. Letter of William III, August 12, 1689, in Moody & Simmons, *Selected Documents*, p. 176. The revolutionary government immediately ordered that the King's letter be published to ensure judicial judgements would be respected; and that government edicts would be obeyed. (See Orders of the Convention, December 3 and 16, in *ibid*, pp. 179-180 & 185-186.

51. "Resolution of the Convention", January 24, 1690, in *ibid*, p. 197.

52. General Court Order, January 4, 1690, in *ibid*, pp. 202-203. Ultimately Sir Edmund Andros and his councillors were exonerated and set free as the Massachusetts government's agents in London refused to sign the colony's indictment for fear of being sued, and held personally responsible for financial damages, should the charges not be upheld in court. See R. Johnson, *Adjustment to Empire*, pp. 171-173.

53. "Declaration published in Boston by the Governor in Council and Representatives", December 16, 1689, in Moody & Simmons, *Selected Documents*, pp. 185-186.

54. *Ibid*; and M. Halsey Thomas, ed., *The Diary of Samuel Sewall, Vol. I, 1674-1729* (New York: Farrar, Straus and Giroux, 1973), p. 291.

55. On the evolution of the negotiations over the terms of the new charter, see R. Johnson, *Adjustment to Empire*, pp. 205-239; and Moody & Simmons, *Selected Documents*, "Historical Introduction", pp. 27-41. Arguments against restoring the Charter of 1629, and the extent to which the Puritans were alleged to have usurped powers under the Charter, engaged in illegal acts, and arbitrarily violated the rights of non-Puritans, were enumerated in a number of reports prepared for the Lords of Trade and Plantation. See, for example, *ibid*, pp. 489-490, "Considerations concerning the Charter of New England" [c. April 1691]; pp. 491-508, "Reflections on a Pamphlet Lately come abroad, Entitled Reasons for the Confirmation of Charters belonging to the Several Colonies of New England, [c. 1 June], 1691; and pp. 509-510, "Reasons against Restoring the Several Charters of New England are drawn from the Heads following", [1691].

56. "Charter of Massachusetts, 7 October 1691", in Moody and Simmons, *Selected Documents*, pp. 599-620. Two earlier drafts of the charter, and various commentaries by the Massachusetts agents and Crown officials, can be found in *ibid*, p. 524f. See also Lovejoy, *Glorious Revolution*, pp. 346-350; Lewis, "Massachusetts and the Glorious Revolution", pp. 353-355; and Johnson, *Adjustment to Empire*, pp. 229-234. Massachusetts was the only colony where the Assembly was granted the right to elect the Upper House (albeit subject to confirmation by the Governor). Granting the Assembly the right to vote the salary of the Governor and public officials was to prove a gross error on the part of the Crown as it placed an effective weapon in the hands of the Assembly during future power struggles between the legislative and executive branches of the royal government. The new Province of the Massachusetts Bay included Plymouth and Maine, as well as the conquered territory of Acadia.

57. Hutchinson, *The History of Massachusetts*, pp. 349-351 and 34; and *Diary of Samuel Sewall*, entry for May 24, 1682, p. 291. The Council

met on May 24th to proclaim the new royal government and, following an election, the Assembly met for the first time on June 8, 1692. On the establishment of the new royal government see, Emerson W. Baker and John G. Reid, *The New England Knight, Sir William Phips, 1651- 1695* (Toronto: University of Toronto Press, 1998), pp. 178-201.

58. "Governor and Council to Massachusetts Agents", 29 November 1690, in Moody & Simmons, *Selected Documents*, pp. 411-415, and quote p. 412. See also "Humble Address of the Governour and Council and the General Court of Your Majesties Colony of the Massachusetts Bay in New England", [December 1690], *ibid*, pp. 287- 289; and "To the Kings most Excellent Majeste, The Humble Address, of divers of the Gentry Merchants, and others of your Majesties most Loyall and dutyfull subjects Inhabiting in Boston, Charletowne, and places adjacent, within your Majesties Territory and Dominion in New England in America", [January 1691], *ibid*, pp. 416-418.

New England had suffered from a major smallpox epidemic that broke out in October 1689, raged throughout the summer of 1690 killing some 320 persons, and flared up again on smallpox being re-introduced in November 1690 with the return of the soldiers of the Canada expedition . See John Duffy, *Epidemics in Colonial America* (Port Washington, New York: Kennaket Press, 1953), p. 48.

During the period 1691-1692, the French and their Indian allies were pre-occupied in defending Canada, against large Iroquois raiding parties that destroyed and depopulated settlements between Montreal and Trois Rivieres, and in launching retaliatory raids against the Iroquois villages, north of Albany. The Massachusetts Bay Colony settlements on the northern frontier were spared from French attacks; although the threat remained of a renewal of the devastating raids of 1689-1690, which had caused so much loss of life, destruction of property, and spread sheer terror among the New England frontier settlements. (See Eccles, *Canada under Louis XIV, 1663-1701*, pp.185- 193.

59. Francis Hill, *A Delusion of Satan: The Full Story of the Salem Witch Trials* (New York: Doubleday, 1998). As Perry Miller has asserted, the hysteria of the Salem witch trials is quite "intelligible within the logic of the covenant". (See Miller, *From Colony to Province*, pp. 180-195,

and especially pp. 191-192). There was also a connection between the witchcraft phenomenon and the terrors of the frontier Indian warfare, see Baker & Reid, *The New England Knight*, pp. 134-155, and especially, pp. 142-143. A substantial number of the accusers, judges, and accused, in the Salem witch trials were persons who had suffered losses of family and/or property in Indian attacks.

60. "Governor and Council to Massachusetts Agents", 29 November 1690, in Moody and Simmons, *Selected Documents*, pp. 411-418; and "To the Kings most Excellent Majesty, The Petition of Severall Merchants and others who have concerns in New England", [April 1691], *ibid*, p. 478.

61. The modern concept of sovereignty as singular, indivisible, and absolute raises a seeming paradox where a sovereign state is limited by international law and international courts. However, these restrictions are auto limitations. In effect, limitations that the sovereign state agrees to accept. This was the case with the revolutionary popular government of the Massachusetts Bay Colony. It was established on the basis of popular sovereignty, but the representatives of the people in adopting the annulled charter of 1629 as the constitution for their new government agreed to accept the requirement of the Charter of 1629 that no laws be passed contrary to the laws of England; and the revolutionary government of its own freewill professed its allegiance and loyalty to the English Crown. Theorists argue that an independent sovereign state remains fully sovereign despite the existence of such self-imposed, or consensual limitations. (See "Political Science: The doctrine of sovereignty", *Encylopaedia Britannica*, 15th. ed., vol. 14 (1980), p. 703).

62. When palatine powers were granted to a vassal-in-chief in feudal land grants in return for allegiance and military support in defending the king's realm, the military obligations were customarily specified in the grant, as well as any limitations that the king wanted to impose on the vassal's right to make war and peace. However, the right to make war conveyed in the grant of palatine powers was not necessarily limited to the territory of the palatinate. The Carolina Charter of 1663 granted the proprietors the right "to make war and pursue the enemies aforesaid [savages, other enemies, pirates and robbers], as well

by sea as by land, yea, even without the limits of the said province". However, the revolutionary popular government of the Massachusetts Bay territory was a sovereign power until superseded by a restored royal government. It was established on the basis of popular sovereignty, and when subsequently recognized and empowered to act for the Crown no specific limits were placed on the exercise of that power. Hence the revolutionary popular government, in its function as a provisional government, possessed the sovereign right to make war beyond its territory in defence of the king's realm.

63. See, for example, General Court Minutes, June 6, 7, 12, 14 and 19, and July 4, 1690, in Moody & Simmons, *Selected Documents*, pp. 248, 249, 251-252, and 262-263, for the wording of the acts of the General Court that authorized the Canada Expedition, the requisitioning and recruitment of the men, ships, munitions and supplies for the expedition, and the appointment of Sir William Phips to command.

64. Articles of War in the "Journal of Lt. General John Walley of the expedition to Canada", November 27, 1690, reprinted in Walter K. Watkins, *Soldiers in the Expedition to Canada in 1690, and Grantees of the Canada Townships* (Boston: Printed by the Author, 1898), pp. 7-9.

65. Phips" ultimatum, reprinted in Mather, *The Life of Sir William Phips*, p. 73.

66. As of 1690 the Congregationalist Church was well established in the Massachusetts Bay Colony, and the former Puritans of the Church of England were congregationalists in terms of their religious adherence. However, herein the concern is with Puritanism as a world view and a religious frame of mind, rather than with their particular church affiliation at any given time. Hence, the continued use of the phrase "Massachusetts Puritans" and "Puritans".

67. This is all by way of saying, from a historian's perspective, that ideas do influence actions; and that the historian in seeking to understand the deeper motives and rationale underlying a historical event, must probe the mindset of the historical actors.

Bibliography

Primary Sources - Published

[*The*] *Andros Tracts, Being a Collection of Pamphlets and Official Papers*, Vol. III, with Notes by W.H. Whitmore. New York: Burt Franklin, 1874.

Canada, *Canadian Archives Report, 1912*, Sessional Paper No. 29b, Appendix E, pp. 54-63, "Journal of the Expedition under Sir William Phips against Port Royal, 1690", April 23, 1690- May 16, 1690", and pp. 64-66, "An Abstract of a Lre from Mr. James Lloyd, Mercht in Boston", January 8, 1690/91; and *ibid*, Appendix G, pp. 75-78, "Letter from Captain Nicholson written from James City, Virginia, to the Lords of Trade and Plantations", November 4, 1690.

Collection des Manuscrits contenant lettres, mémoires et autre documents historiques relatifs à la Nouvelle France, Vol. I. Québec: A. Côté, 1883.

Great Britain, Public Record Office, *Calendar of State Papers, Colonial Series: America and West Indies, January 1693- 14 May 1696*. ed. J.W. Fortescue. London: H.M. Stationery Office, 1903: Paper No. 1,239, p. 389; Paper No. 1,313, p. 385; Paper No. 1314, p. 386; Paper No. 1315, p. 387; and Paper No. 1417, p. 415.

Hall, Michael G., Lawrence H. Leder, & Michael G. Kammen, eds., *The Glorious Revolution in America: Documents on the Colonial Crisis of 1689*. Chapel Hill: University of North Carolina Press, 1964.

Mather, Cotton. *The Life of Sir William Phips*. ed. Mark Van Doren. New York: AMS Press, 1919, 1st. ed. 1797.

Moody, Robert Earle & Richard Clive Simmons, eds., *The Glorious Revolution in Massachusetts, Selected Documents 1689-1692*. Boston: The Colonial Society of Massachusetts, 1988.

Thomas, M. H. ed., *The Diary of Samuel Sewall, Vol. I, 1674-1708*. New York: Farrar, Straus and Giroux, 1973.

Wise, John. *Two Narratives of the Expedition against Quebec, A.D. 1690, Under Sir William Phips*. ed. Samuel A. Green. Cambridge: John Wilson and Son, 1902.

Secondary Sources - Books

Baker, Emerson W. & John G. Reid, *The New England Knight, Sir William Phips, 1651-1695*. Toronto: University of Toronto Press, 1998.

Beer, George L. *The Origins of the British Colonial System, 1578-1660*. New York: Macmillan Company, 1922.

Carlton, Charles. *Archbishop William Laud*. London: Rutledge & Kegan Paul, 1987.

Duffy, John. *Epidemics in Colonial America*. Port Washington, New York: Kennikat Press, 1972.

Eccles, W.J. *Canada Under Louis XIV, 1663-1701*. Toronto: McClelland and Stewart, 1964.

Johnson, Paul. *A History of the American People*. London: Orion Books, 1998.

Johnson, Richard R. *Adjustment to Empire, The New England Colonies, 1675-1715*. New Brunswick, New Jersey: Rutgers University Press, 1981.

Bibliography

Johnson, Richard R. *John Nelson, Merchant Adventurer, A Life Between Empires.* London: Oxford University Press, 1991.

Jones, J.R. *The Revolution of 1688 in England.* London: Weidenfeld & Nicolson, 1972.

Ku, Charlotte & Paul F. Diehl, eds., *International Law, Classic and Contemporary Readings.* Boulder, Colorado: Lynne Rienner Publishers Inc., 1998.

Hall, Michael G. *The Last American Puritan: the life of Increase Mather, 1639-1723.* Middleton, Connecticut: Wesleyan University Press, 1988.

Hill, Francis. *A Delusion of Satan: The Full Story of the Salem Witch Trials.* New York: Doubleday, 1998.

Hutchinson, Thomas. *The History of the Colony and Province of Massachusetts-bay*, ed. Lawrence Shaw Mayo. Cambridge, Massachusetts: Harvard University Press, 1936. (Reprint of vol. I, 1764, vol. II, 1767, and of unpublished manuscript of vol. III.)

Lanctot, Gustave. *A History of Canada, Vol. 2, From the Royal Régime to the Treaty of Utrecht, 1663-1713.* Toronto: Clarke, Irwin & Co., 1964.

Lovejoy, David S. *The Glorious Revolution in America.* New York: Harper & Row Publishers, 1972.

Malone, Patrick M. *The Skulking Way of War: Technology and Tactics among the New England Indians.* Baltimore: John Hopkins University Press, 1991.

Miller, Perry. *Errand into the Wilderness.* New York: Harper Torchbooks, 1964.

Miller, Perry. *The New England Mind, From Colony to Province.* Cambridge, Mass.: Harvard University Press, 1962.

Morgan, Edmund S. *The Puritan Dilemma, The Story of John Winthrop.* ed. by Oscar Handlin. Boston: Little, Brown and Company, 1958.

Mosse, George L. *The Struggle for Sovereignty in England, From the Reign of Queen Elizabeth to the Petition of Right.* New York: Octagon Books, 1950, reprinted 1968.

Myrand, Ernest. *Sir William Phips Devant Québec, Histoire d'un siege.* Quebec: Demers, 1893.

Ogg, David. *Louis XIV.* 2nd. ed. London: Oxford University Press, 1967.

Oldmixon, John. *The British Empire in America containing the history of the discovery, settlement, progress and present state of all the British Colonies on the continent and islands of America.* Vol. I. London: J. Nicholson, B. Tooke, 1708, microfilm, 1969.

Orcutt, William Dana. *Good Old Dorchester, A Narrative History of the Town, 1630-1893.* Cambridge: Published by Author, 1893.

Pencak, William. *War, politics, and revolution in provincial Massachusetts.* Boston: Northeastern University Press, 1981.

Parkman, Francis. *Count Frontenac and New France under Louis XIV.* Toronto: George N. Morang & Co., 1899.

Parkman, Francis. *France and England in North America.* Vol. II. New York: The Library of America, 1983. (1st edition 1884.)

Pinkham, Lucille. *William III and the Respectable Revolution.* Cambridge: Harvard University Press, 1954.

Proulx, Gilles. *Between France and New France, Life Aboard the Tall Sailing Ships.* Toronto: Dundurn Press, 1984.

Rohr, John von. *The Covenent of Grace in Puritan Thought* . Atlanta, Georgia: Scholars Press, 1986.

Sabine, George H. *A History of Political Theory.* 3rd. ed. New York: Holt, Rineholt & Winston, 1961.

Stubbs, William. *The Constitutional History of England, in Its Origin and Development.* Vol. I. New York: Barnes & Noble, 6th ed., 1967.

Stubbs, William. *The Constitutional History of England, in its Origin and Development.* Vol. III. Oxford: Clarendon Press, 1878.

Tuchman, Barbara W. *Practicing History, Selected Essays.* New York: Alfred A. Knopf, 1981.

Watkins, Walter K. *Soldiers in the Expedition to Canada in 1690, and Grantees of the Canada Townships.* Boston: Printed by the Author, 1898.

Secondary Sources - Articles

Baker, Emerson W. & John G. Reid, "Amerindian Power in the Early Moderns Northeast: A Reappraisal", *William and Mary Quarterly*, vol. LXI, No. 1, (January 2004), pp. 77-106.

"Congregationalists", *Encylopaedia Britannica*, 15th ed., vol. 4, (1980), pp. 1127-1130.

Haffenden, Philip S. "The Crown and the Colonial Charters, 1675-1688", *William and Mary Quarterly*, XIV, Part I (July 1958), pp. 297-311, and Part II (October 1958), pp. 452-466.

"Political Science: The doctrine of sovereignty", *Encylopaedia Britannica*, 15th. ed., vol. 14, (1980), p. 703.

"Puritanism", *Encylopaedia Britannica*, 15th ed. , vol. 15 (1980), pp. 304-308.

Thesis

Lewis, Theodore B. jr. "Massachusetts and the Glorious Revolution". Ph.D. dissertation, University of Wisconsin, 1967.

Index

Acadia Expedition
    Appeal to King William, 10
    Appointment of Phips, 5, 8-9, 10
    Attack on Port Royal, 11
    Cost of, 12
    Inception, 4
    Financing, 4-5
    Fleet of Phips, 27
    French prisoners, 11-12, 19, 30
    Invasion force, 60
    Plunder, 11-12
    Recruitment, 5-6

Albany, 10-11, 36

Andros, Sir Edmund, 3, 99-100, 124, 135, 140

Bradstreet, Simon, 9, 20-21, 23, 101

Cambridge Platform, 87-88

Canada Expedition Organization
    Appeal to Rhode Island, 19
    Appointment of Phips, 13-14, 16
    Clerical exhortations, 18
    Defensive war concept, 19, 30
    Division of plunder plan, 15
    Fleet composition, 22, 24, 31
    Gunpowder shortage, 16, 22, 29, 31
    Inception, 4, 10, 12-13
    Impressments of ships, 13-16
    Merchant subscriptions, 22
    Militia recruitment, 14-15, 18-19, 28-29
    Militia strength, 23-24, 36
    Overland Expedition, 37-38

Purpose of, 4, 9-10, 20- 21
Tax Levy, 19
Two-pronged attack, 11, 37

Canada Expedition and Quebec
    Arrival at Tadoussac, 39
    Arrival at Quebec, 39
    Articles of War, 38-39
    Departure from Boston, 38
    French forces at Montreal, 39, 40, 46
    French forces at Quebec, 39, 40, 46, 47
    French skirmishers, 42-43, 45, 47
    French strategy, 45-46
    Gunpowder and munitions, 43, 44, 46
    Île d'Orléans, 48-49, 67
    Landing on Beauport Shore, 41-44
    New England casualties, 42
    Plan of attack, 40-41
    Phips' Ultimatum, 40-41, 65, 66, 77
    Quebec bombardment, 43-44, 46, 67
    St. Charles River, 41, 43-46
    Walley's advance, 43-44, 67
    Walley's dilemma, 46-47
    Weather, 39-40, 42, 45, 49-50
    Withdrawal, 47-50
    Tides, 41- 43, 45, 48

Canada Expedition Aftermath
    Anticosti Island, 52
    Appeal to King, 53
    Cannibalism, 70
    Colonial defence, 56
    Deaths, 51-52, 68-70
    Debt of Massachusetts, 53, 71
    Discharge of public debt, 54-59, 71
    Division of plunder plan, 50
    Invasion force, 60-61
    Land grants, 73

Index

　　　Lost ships, 51-52, 59
　　　Paper bills of credit, 54-55
　　　Payments for lost ships, 58-59
　　　Pay of troops, 15, 28, 53-54, 58
　　　Pensions and Care, 58, 61
　　　Protestant victories in Europe, 57, 73-73
　　　Return voyage, 49, 50-52
　　　Role of Massachusetts, 60-61
　　　Role of the Crown, 53, 60-61
　　　Spring of 1691 recovery, 57
　　　Taxes levied, 50, 55-57, 64, 68, 70-71
　　　Tax collection, 56, 68, 71
　　　Weather, 40, 42, 45, 49-50, 52
　　　West Indies, 50, 52

Canadien militia, 40, 42, 45, 47-48

Carr, Edward Hallett, xviii

Catholic Counter-Reformation, 84, 136

Cavalier Parliament, 87, 129-131

Clarendon Code, 130-131

Colonial Defence
　　　Albany, 36
　　　French warships, 36
　　　Frontiers, 3-4, 9-10, 35-36, 56
　　　Maine, 36, 64
　　　Role of Crown, 3, 19-21, 36, 60-61
　　　'Skulking' warfare, 35, 63

Connecticut Colony, 10, 37

Convention Parliament (England), 7, 104

Cromwell, Oliver, 86

153

Danforth, Thomas, 23

Divine Providence, 56-57, 60, 72, 83, 114-115, 123

Dudley, Joseph, 97

Duke of York (James II), 87

French-Indian Raids
    Fort Loyal (Falmouth), 29, 36
    Maine, 36
    New England, 35-36
    Pemaquid (Bristol), Maine, 36, 63
    Quochecho (Dover), New Hampshire, 63
    Salmon Falls, New Hampshire, 9, 27, 63
    Schenectady, New York, 5, 63

French Invasion Plan, 64

Gallop, Captain Samuel, 52

Glorious Revolution of 1688, 7, 99, 103-104

Great Ejection in England, 87, 129-131

Kings of England
Charles I (1625-1649), 81-82, 86, 91
Charles II (1660-1685), 87, 94, 97
James II (1685-1688), 87, 97, 99-100, 135
William III (1689-1702), 95-96, 100-104, 108-111

Iroquois raids
    La Chesnaye, 25
    Lachine, 25
    Laprarie, 37-38

Julian calendar, 62

Massachusetts
- Annulment of the Charter, 96-97, 134, 141
- Arminianism, 82-83, 128
- Cambridge Platform (1648), 87-88, 131-132
- Charter of 1629, 81-82, 85, 88-91, 96-97, 120
- Charter of 1691, 111-113, 141
- City upon a Hill, 84, 123
- Convention of 1689, 103-105
- Council for Safety, 101-103, 136
- Covenant of Grace, 83-84, 90-91
- Colonial defence, 86-87
- Declaration of Liberties & Rights, 88-90
- Dominion of New England, 3, 97-98
- Dudley administration, 97
- English Civil War (1642-1651), 86
- Episcopal ordination, 84, 13180
- Founding Puritans, 81-85
- Form of government, 84-86
- Holy War, 84
- Insurrection of April 1689, 98-103, 136
- Interregnum, 116-120
- Laws of England, 81, 106-117
- Laws of Scripture, 85, 103, 123
- Loyalty Address, 101-102
- Navigations Acts, 95-96, 134
- Oath of Allegiance, 85-86, 89-90, 107, 110
- Predestination, 82-84
- Provisional government, 108-110
- Puritan theology, 82-84
- Republican interregnums, 86, 98-102
- Revoking the Charter, 96-97
- Revolutionary popular government, 104-108, 143
- Royal authority, 84-87, 95-98, 117-118, 121-122, 124-125
- Salem witch trials, 114-115, 142-143
- Settlement purpose, 82
- Stuart restoration (1660), 86-87, 94-95

Mather, Reverend Cotton, 8, 9

Mather, Reverend Increase, 7-8, 101, 109, 113

Militia Companies
    Dorchester, viii, 51, 70
    Roxbury, 51-52, 70
    Rowley, 51-52
    Plymouth, 10, 51, 68

Miller, Perry, xiii-xiv, xvi

New Haven, 87

New York Colony, 10, 36-38

Newel, Samuel, 52, 70

Parks Canada
    Shipwreck project, vii
    Shipwreck identification, viii
    Research project, vii-viii

Phips, Sir William
    Appointment (Acadia Expedition), 5
    Appointment (Canada Expedition), 13-14
    Early life, 5-10
    Royal Governor, 113, 115
    Ultimatum at Quebec, 39-41, 65-66, 125

Plymouth Colony, 11, 29

Port Royal, 4, 11

Prince of Orange (William III), 7, 99-100, 108-111

Protestant Succession (England), 103-104

Index

Protestantism in Europe
    Year 1629, 128
    Year 1685, 137-138

Rainsford, Captain John, 52

Savage, Captain Ephraim, 42

Schuyler, Captain John, 37-38

Ships
    Adventure of Captain William Bradlow, 51
    American Merchant of Captain Joseph Eldridge, 24
    Boston Merchant of Captain William Shute, 51
    Elizabeth and Mary of Captain Caleb Lamb, viii, 51, 59
    John and Thomas of Captain Thomas Carter, 17, 24
    Hannah and Mary of Captain Thomas Parker, 51, 59
    Mary of Captain John Rainsford, 51, 59
    Mary Ann of Captain Gregory Sugar, jr., 51, 59
    Six Friends (Flagship), 22, 24, 36, 38, 42
    Swan of Captain Thomas Gilbert, 24, 36

Smallpox, 19, 29, 37, 40, 47, 50-51, 57, 65, 68-69, 70, 142

Sovereignty
    Absolute in France, 135, 137
    Papal concept of, 135
    Canada Expedition, 118-120, 125
    Carolina Palatine charters (1663, 1665), 93-94, 133-134
    Corporate charters, 79-81, 134
    Declaration of Liberties & Rights (June 1661), 88-91
    Divine Right of Kings, 129
    Feudal concept, 78, 132
    Maryland Palatine charter (1632), 91-93, 133
    Dispute in Massachusetts, 84-87, 88-95, 118-120, 125
    Modern indivisible concept of, 74, 143
    Palatine powers, 78, 117-118, 121, 123, 132-133, 143-144
    Palatine charters, 78

Popular sovereignty, 104-105, 107, 110, 139
Sovereignty in the 17th Century, 77-78, 135, 139
Struggle in England, 129
Royal Sovereignty, 3, 77-81, 118-120

Tadoussac, 38, 49, 67-68, 119

Toleration
    Act of Toleration (England), 131
    Carolina charter of 1663, 133-134
    Puritan rejection of, 88, 133-134
    Peace of Westphalia (1648), 137-138

Tuchman, Barbara, xiv-xv

Wabanaki, 3, 6, 56-57, 115

Walley, Lt. Gen. John, 24, 42-48, 67

Westminster Confession of Faith (1647), 87, 131

Winthrop, John, 84

Wise, Reverend John, 43, 46

A Note About the Author

Robert W. Passfield was born and raised in St. Thomas, Ontario, Canada. He is a graduate of the University of Western Ontario (Honours BA, History, 1968), and McMaster University (MA History, 1969), and pursued Ph.D. studies at McMaster University where he read in a major field, Canadian History (Pre- and Post-Confederation), and three minor fields (Political Philosophy, Modern European History, and Diplomatic History). With his dissertation incomplete, he joined the Parks Canada Programme of the Department of Indian Affairs and Northern Development in Ottawa as an historical researcher in the National Historic Sites Branch.

You become what you do! During a 30-year career as a public historian Passfield worked in a variety of fields: industrial archaeology; history of technology; engineering history; and heritage conservation. He read widely in all of these fields, and prepared numerous reports recording, documenting, and evaluating the heritage value of engineering works in support of the heritage conservation mandate of Parks Canada. He was also called upon to prepare Agenda Papers and Submission Reports documenting and evaluating the historical significance of prominent Canadian persons, places, and events in support of the national commemoration mandate of the Historic Sites and Monuments Board of Canada.

Passfield has published a number of articles in professional journals, two books on heritage canals, and has contributed chapters to several books in public works history. In 1987 he was awarded the Norton Prize (now the Robert M. Vogel Prize) by the Society for Industrial Archeology (SIA) for an outstanding article in industrial archaeology, and in 1996 the W. Gordon Plewes Award by the Canadian Society for Civil Engineering (CSCE) for a noteworthy contribution to Canadian engineering history. He has also received a Parks Canada Merit Award and a Parks Canada Prix d'Excellence for his contributions to Parks Canada programme initiatives. Most of his publications are an offshoot of research reports prepared in support of the Parks Canada heritage conservation mandate, and the national commemoration mandate of the Historic Sites and Monuments Board of Canada.

In retirement, Passfield has continued to work as a historian in the fields of research pursued during his professional career, and in 2010 was granted the status of Senior Historian Emeritus by the Parks Canada Agency for his distinguished past service, and his continued support of Parks Canada in mentoring new staff members and acting in a corporate memory capacity. Passfield is a member of the Society for the History of Technology (SHOT), the Society for Industrial Archeology (SIA), and the Canadian Science and Technology Historical Association (CSTHA).

Printed in Great Britain
by Amazon